John Jacobs, 1951.

50 YEARS
OF GOLFING WISDOM

JOHN JACOBS
WITH STEVE NEWELL

CollinsWillow

An Imprint of HarperCollins*Publishers*

First published in 2005 by
Collins Willow
an imprint of HarperCollins*Publishers*
London

© John Jacobs and Steve Newell 2005

1

A CIP catalogue record for this book is
available from the British Library

ISBN 0 00 719393 9

Illustrations by Rob Davies

Set in 11/14 pt Linotype Sabon by
Rowland Phototypesetting Ltd, Bury St Edmunds, Suffolk

Printed and bound in Great Britain by
Clays Ltd, St Ives plc

The HarperCollins website address is
www.harpercollins.co.uk

Contents

Foreword

Nothing meaningful in this life is ever achieved without hard work, but one always needs a little bit of luck. John Jacobs deserves his success in golf, because he invested plenty of the former and, as he freely admits, was blessed with a little of the latter, too. His talent took care of the rest. His journey is extraordinary.

John started his professional golfing life in his father's shop at Lindrick Golf Club in Yorkshire. He would stoke the fires in the grate on Monday mornings to burn out the snapped hickory shafts of clubs broken over the course of a weekend's play. He grew up to become one of golf's most influential figures – tournament winner, undefeated Ryder Cup player, captain of the Ryder Cup team, founder of the PGA Tour, OBE, past President of the PGA of Europe, a member of golf's exclusive Hall of Fame and also the Teaching Hall of Fame (itself a rare double honour), and winner of the prestigious Geoffrey Dyson Award for Sporting Teaching Excellence in 2002. Most recently Jacobs was awarded honorary membership of the R&A. The list could go on further, were there space.

Above all, though, John Jacobs is one of golf's all-time

great teachers – a true legend of the game who is in the unique position of having taught hundreds of thousands of amateurs around the world how to play better golf, in-between passing on his words of wisdom to the world's greatest players of the last 50 years. No other coach has had more success in making the best even better. The same could be said for his influence on today's leading coaches.

John himself is far too modest to even suggest that a list of tributes from great players through the years be included in this book, but as his collaborator on this project I am happy to relieve him of this burden, for I think it is entirely appropriate that within the remit of this foreword there is scope for personal contributions which put in perspective John's impact on the game of golf.

'It is an unrelenting insistence on understanding and applying the fundamental objectives of the swing, plus his remarkable ability to explain them clearly, that makes John Jacobs such a great golf teacher. Because his logic is unarguable and his reasoning so understandable, his success rate with all levels of golfers from beginner to tournament player has been and continues to be outstanding.'

Jack Nicklaus

'John Jacobs has been a friend of mine for many years. He is an outstanding teacher and has also been an excellent golfer and a fierce competitor on the course. However, of greatest importance for me is that he is a true gentleman and an asset to the game.' *Gary Player*

'John Jacobs has contributed a great deal to the game and he is considered one of golf's premier teachers. In building my own career, he was certainly one of the instructors I studied and he has an outstanding ability to analyse golfers' problems through their ball flight. He is one of the game's real grandmasters.' *David Leadbetter*

'John is the nicest person I have met in my 25-year amateur and professional career. He really is a true friend. As a golf teacher he is without doubt The Master. Simplicity is the word I would use to describe his teaching. His theories on the golf swing and the lessons he gives are so crystal clear and understandable that he makes the game of golf seem easy. His advice helps bring better golf within everyone's grasp.' *Jose Maria Olazabal*

'I was just 14 when I first saw John Jacobs on the practice ground at Dalmahoy. It was not his swing that caught my eye, or the way he addressed the ball, but rather the fact that he never had time to practise himself because so many of his colleagues kept asking for advice. As always it was given freely. John remains the supreme enthusiast gaining his pleasure from helping fellow pros and amateurs – thousands over the years – play the game better and enjoy it more. I seek out John two or three times a year to have a look at my swing and he has never let me down. Come to think of it, I'd question whether he has ever let anyone down.' *Bernard Gallacher*

'The two biggest influences are my dad and John Jacobs. I like the way John talks about the swing path all the time. The way he makes everything very simple and straight-forward – that's the way I like to teach.' *Butch Harmon*

'John's achievements are endless as a player, teacher, writer, communicator, golf course designer, and executive director of the men's European Tour. I can think of no better host, or better companion.'   *Mickey Walker*

John Jacobs isn't just a great teacher, though. He could play a bit himself and was, at times, good enough to beat the best. He competed in the Ryder Cup and won tournaments, including the Dutch Open in 1957 and a memorable victory over Grand Slam winner Gary Player, in the final of the South African Matchplay Championship.

John had an equally significant influence on the administration of the game, having been instrumental in setting up what is now the European Tour. Indeed, John sees this as perhaps his greatest achievement, a view endorsed by Mark McCormack in his *World of Professional Golf Annual* in 1973. McCormack wrote of the haphazard affair that constituted the British Pro golf scene and the plan devised by John Jacobs to overcome the crisis situation.

'The Jacobs plan worked. The crowds did come back. Public interest was reawakened. And the ultimate proof that golf was back in favour was that both the BBC and the independent companies returned coverage of PGA tournaments to their schedules. The outlook for pro golf, which had seemed so desolate twelve months previously, had taken a decided turn for the better. The mood among the players was buoyant. Golf had begun to believe in itself again. I for one do not doubt that 1972 was a year of high significance. It might be no more than slight exaggeration to say that these twelve months saw British golf progress by a quarter of a century. And that is quite a trick.'

John has also authored numerous bestselling books on how to play the game, many of which are still considered benchmark manuals, revered and studied decades after they first went into print. For the record, these include:

Golf, first published in 1963, with a foreword by Laddie Lucas. This was made up of a collection of articles which first appeared in the pages of *Golfing* magazine during the late 1950s and early 1960s.

Play Better Golf, published in 1969, based on the manuscripts from the hugely popular Yorkshire TV series of the same name. John made a series of thirteen 30-minute programmes, followed by two further series, during which time the director suggested he write a book to go with it. It went on to sell well over half-a-million copies.

Practical Golf, first published in 1972 with a foreword by Tony Jacklin, went on to become a bestseller. John considers it 'the most important book I wrote.' It contained many articles from the first ten years of *Golf World* and was compiled by that magazine's editor Ken Bowden, who later went on to edit *Golf Digest* in the US and write much of Jack Nicklaus' published work.

John Jacobs Analyses Golf's Superstars, published in 1974, in collaboration with Ken Bowden. This was perhaps the first book of its type, focusing as it did on the swings of the leading players of the day, with analysis from John and words of wisdom to help the average golfer learn from the greats.

Golf Doctor was first published in 1979 and entitled *Curing Faults for Weekend Golfers* in the US editions (a title which incidentally killed it from a sales perspective, because people thought it was simply a band aid), with a foreword by Jack Nicklaus and co-written with Dick Aultman. John says he wrote this as much for the pro to teach, as for the pupils. However it is interpreted, there is no doubt that a quarter of a century after it first went into print, it remains golf's ultimate 'self help' manual.

The Golf Swing Simplified, first published in 1993 and again co-written by Ken Bowden, was a wonderfully succinct study of the golf swing, devoted to its most critical component: the action required to strike the ball most effectively from the tee and then on to the green.

Golf in a Nutshell, first published in 1995, was written with the legendary golf journalist Peter Dobereiner. This project came about when Dobereiner wrote an article in *Golf Digest* magazine praising the talents of John Jacobs and highlighting the merits of *Practical Golf*, the best-selling golf book of all time until Harvey Penick's *Little Red Book*. John suggested to Peter that they write their own little red book . . . and this was it.

The 50 Greatest Golf Lessons of the 20th Century is John's most recent book, published in 1999, which I had the pleasure of collaborating on. Rather in the style of John's earlier book on golf's superstars, this work featured a biography on the great golfers of the 20th century with insightful analysis from John on the way they played the game and how we mere mortals can benefit.

This is an appropriate moment to go right back to the start, though, to John's first ever instruction book, *Golf*, for it was in the foreword that John's good friend and former Walker Cup captain Laddie Lucas wrote: 'John teaches the skilled and the average, the illustrious and the humble, with a success which has earned him, deservedly, the pseudonym 'Dr Golf'. I have a feeling that this substantial treatise is only the forerunner of what may flow from this fertile mind.' How prophetic that statement proved to be.

Now for the first time ever, the collective works of John's books, as listed above, are brought together in this one volume – *50 Years of Golfing Wisdom*. It's the best of the best, in every sense. It represents an unmissable opportunity for golfers of all abilities to benefit from one of the keenest, wisest, most knowledgeable minds in golf.

50 Years of Golfing Wisdom includes all of the lessons and advice that made John the original, and many say still the ultimate, golfing guru. Where appropriate, we've even included contemporary drawings from the relevant book. Every department of the game receives the Jacobs treatment – in other words, simple, easy to understand, effective advice on how to maximize your potential and play your best golf. From the fundamentals, to problem solving, and curing your bad shots, to instruction on hitting every shot from the longest drive to the most testing putt, and everything in between. There are also studies of some of the great players in history and what you can learn from them.

50 Years of Golfing Wisdom is so comprehensive, so packed full of good advice, it may just be the only instruction book you'll ever need. As Tony Jacklin said in the foreword to *Practical Golf*, 'Putting golf technique down on paper is extremely difficult. I think Jacobs does it superbly. This book is a wonderful distillation of an exceptional man's knowledge, and I don't see how it can fail to help any golfer play better.' My sentiments exactly.

Steve Newell

A Lifetime's Philosophy*

Golf is what the ball does, which is totally dependent upon what the club is doing at impact. The variants at impact are:

The clubface: which can be open, closed or square (strong or weak).
The swing path: which can be in-to-out, out-to-in, or straight.
The angle of attack: which can be too steep, too shallow, or correct for the individual club.
The clubhead speed: to suit the shot in hand.

These dimensions, the clubface, swing path, and angle of attack, all of which determine the flight of the ball, are very influenced by the set-up at address.

The grip has a direct bearing on clubface control at impact.

---

* An extract from the *2003 PGA Golf Coaching – Swing Manual*, reproduced with kind courtesy of the Professional Golfers Association, GB&I.

The clubface aim and body alignment has a direct bearing on the swing path at impact.

The body posture at address has a direct bearing on the degree of shoulder tilt during the body turn, affecting the swing plane and therefore the angle of attack at impact. This does not mean that everyone will set up to the ball in exactly the same way. As teachers, prescribing the correct set-up for the individual is our greatest teaching tool.

Turning to the swing itself, which is conditioned by the position of the ball relative to the player, which is to the side and on the ground. The fact that it is to the side requires the club to swing through the ball from the inside back to the inside with the swing path on line at impact, with the clubface square to that line. The correct body action facilitates this arc of swing.

Since the ball is on the ground, at the same time as the body turns, the hands and arms swing the club up, down and up again in unison with the body action.

The above, I believe, is applicable to every player, allowing for individual variations.

The shape of a golf lesson would normally take the form of: diagnosis, explanation accompanied by demonstration and finally, correction. The pupil is best viewed down the line to facilitate this approach. The set-up to the target can be observed and the subsequent swing path through the ball can be clearly seen. The flight of the ball relative to the swing path will give a valid indication of the clubface at impact. This is not to say the side view for players of all levels is on occasion very appropriate.

It is vital that the correct diagnosis is made and that the explanation and accompanying demonstration be fully understood by the pupil in order to encourage the necessary perseverance since any correction is likely to be, initially, uncomfortable.

Understanding Golf's Fundamentals

On reading golf

One reason, I have always thought, why golf can become such a difficult game is simply because there are so many different ways of playing it correctly; and that one secret, for any golfer striving to improve, is to decide first which is his or her own correct way. It is my sincere hope that this book will help any reader to do just that.

The correct way, I'm firmly convinced, is invariably the simplest. What may prove simple to one, though, may not necessarily be simple to another. One of the difficulties in studying golf in books lies in learning to select from other people's experiences, ideas and theories, and adapt them to your own personal needs. I think I have found truth in almost every book or article I have read on golf! Yet, in spite of that fact, there is often one thing or another in any particular book which, read by the wrong person, could cause a real setback in his or her game.

As an illustration of this I remember two ladies, both good performers around 8-handicap, who arrived for tuition. Both were accustomed to playing together. One lady hooked her shots, the other sliced. Here were two ladies with faults that I must tell each other to copy! I wanted each to try to do precisely what was wrong in the other! In other words, my instruction was of a completely contradictory nature.

It had to go even further than that, though. Needing contrasting advice, it followed that since they were both avid readers on golf, they also needed different advice on what to read. I told Lady No.1 with her too-flat swing and hook, to read Byron Nelson's book, because he was an upright swinger; and Lady No.2, with her too-upright swing and slice, to read Ben Hogan's, because he was a rounded swinger. *This was 50 years ago, of course. Today, I might replace these two role models with, say, Colin Montgomerie (upright) and Ian Woosnam (rounded).*

The point I'm trying to make is that it is as well to appreciate what we are doing wrong before we seek remedies by reading, from no matter how impeccable a source. The golfing public has been saturated with golf books, most of which have been very good, in many ways. I feel, however, that the titles have been wrong. Most of them should have been called *How I Play Golf* – and how the writer of each book plays golf may not be the easiest way to teach each of his readers.

I sincerely hope that this book will make it easier for you to decide which is your own best way of playing. As with every lesson I've given, I hope to teach people not just to hit the ball better but to understand *why* they're hitting it better.

Swing, or move from position to position?

Should you really *swing* the club? Or should you merely move through a series of contrived postures, a pattern of carefully thought-out conscious movements, a set of deliberate muscle contortions? The question may seem silly but it is of prime importance, especially if you are new to the game or have never achieved the golfing prowess of which you feel yourself potentially capable.

A Rolls Royce without an engine might look impressive, but it's never going to get out of the garage. In exactly the same way, a golf swing without an engine, however beautifully contoured each part might be, is never going to move the ball very far out of your shadow. To do that, your swing, whatever else it lacks, must have power, motivation. *It must be a swing.* In the simplest of golfing terms, you must 'hit the ball'.

Am I stating the obvious? I think not. Most of the great golfers up to the early 1960s learned the game as caddies. They watched the people they carried for and tried to copy those who played well. They were copying an action, a fluid movement. It would never have occurred to them, even if they had known how, to break the swing down into parts and study it segment by segment in static form. Golf was action, and was learned as such.

Now the camera plays an increasingly large part in the exploration of golf technique, with the result that today a great many people tend to learn golf as a 'static' game rather than as a game of movement. Instead of watching good players in the flesh, and trying to emulate the *action* of a good golf swing, they study static pictures and try to copy the positions in which the camera has frozen the players. They are learning positions which, in themselves, without the essential motivating force of swinging, are almost useless.

This does not mean to say that the very excellent action photographs published in golf magazines and books are of no value in learning the game. But undoubtedly the biggest danger in static golf, in learning from still pictures, is that body action becomes overemphasized. Photographs cannot show motion, but they show very well how the body changes position during the golf swing. It is these positional impressions that the beginner and the poor golfer is apt to copy and frequently overdo.

Body action is important in golf, but is *complementary* to the swinging of the clubhead, not the dominating factor of the swing. The body movement must be in sympathy with the clubhead as controlled by the hands, not try to take over from the clubhead as the function of striking the ball. For the club to swing down and forward at over 100 mph, the arms must swing. Arm and hand action also promote feel, and this too can only be learned by *swinging*.

The grip takes care of the blade

The first thing to understand is that there is no such thing as one single grip, correct for everybody. Men and women with many different grips have all played winning golf. What I try to do is to put a man or woman on to the easiest grip to use with his or her natural swing tendencies.

Any grip that provides for the player to connect with the ball with the blade square to the target at impact while simultaneously allowing for full use of the hands and arms, is correct.

16

If the shots are curving in their flight, even when the stance and swing are right, then the trouble is usually in the grip. Generalizing (and taking no account of special cases), if the ball is curving in its flight through the air towards the left, then the hands are likely to be turned too far over to the right and the correction needed is to move the Vs between thumbs and forefingers inwards past his right shoulder; even, in some cases, until they both point towards his chin, but usually not as far as that.

The converse goes for a man whose shots are curving to the right.

Anywhere between chin and right shoulder can be correct for the Vs, if it works for the player. Experiment helps to find out precisely what is best in every individual case.

Setting up your stance

Most golfers ruin many of their shots before they even begin to swing, simply because they set themselves to the task in the wrong way. It really is absurd for an intelligent person to make no effort to get things right from the start. Yet most golfers don't. And here is one simple way in which they could get a much better grip on their game.

The set-up of a shot can be learnt consciously and without any great mental or physical effort. With a little care and application, any one of us can set up a good swing. Make the effort – and a good swing becomes a probability rather than an impossibility.

a) Stance essentials

1. The first thing to aim is the club-blade, square to the target.
2. Then lines straight through the shoulders and feet should aim approximately parallel, across country, to the line through the clubface to the target.
3. The shoulders must be tilted: that is, the left shoulder must be higher than the right (or vice versa for left-handed golfers).
4. You should never be tense. Your stance should, though, be firm; there should be a feeling of power, almost of the feet trying to grip the ground.
5. The stance is wider for the longer shots than the short shots; approximately shoulder-width for woods, and progressively narrower down to approximately 12 inches for a 9-iron.
6. The way many people take up their stance they might just as well be sitting in a chair, for all the help they get from their feet and legs. The right stance gives one more of a feeling of resting on a tall shooting stick, with the back still fairly straight, and the leg muscles ready for action.

b) Aim and the Shoulders

To me, standing 'open' (body set to make it easier to hit to the left of the target) or 'shut' (to the right of the target) means much more whether the *shoulders* are open or shut, than whether the *feet* are.

If the ball is in the wrong position, the shoulders are likely to be wrongly aligned, whether the feet are correct or not. If the ball is actually too far back, drawing the shoulders to the right, you will then aim to the right with the club as well. Contrarily, a ball too far forward makes you aim to the left. There, quite simply, you have one cause of hundreds of thousands of hooks and slices every weekend!

Basic involuntary hooker's position: ball back, shoulders closed, blade aiming right.

Basic involuntary slicer's position: ball forward, shoulders open, blade aiming left.

Note the cause here of much baffled infuriation: the man who aligns himself to the left of target will then tend to swing across the ball – and slice it to the right! He may then try to correct this by consciously aiming further left; this will probably make him swing even more wildly across it and the ball will slice even more! The converse can just as easily happen to the man who aligns himself to the right of the target.

c) Summing up

At the address, the blade should face the line to the target exactly. The shoulders should be parallel to this line, with the left shoulder higher than the right.

Too simple? Well, may I suggest you take a close look at the address position of the next three weekend golfers you play with. If more than one of them has just these three points of aim correct, then you are obviously playing in very good company!

I'm not saying that the right stance will guarantee a good shot. It won't, of course. But it will make it a great deal easier, just as a wrong stance will make it a great deal more difficult. After all, it is the stance that aims the swing.

Getting it all on track

Picturing a golfer standing on one track of a railway to hit a ball sitting on the other track is one of the most popular teaching analogies. It is used so often because it so perfectly conveys the ideal of aligning one's body parallel to the target line. Such a set-up encourages swinging the clubhead through the ball along, rather than across, the target line. Also note the posture: the golfer bends from the waist with his back straight. His arms hang free and easy. His knees are slightly flexed. Overall, his posture conveys a sense of readiness and resilience.

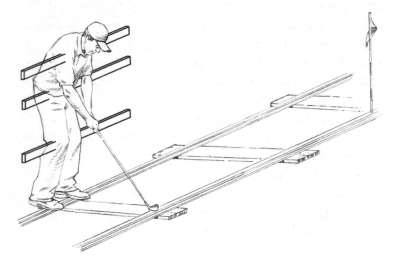

The alignment of the feet, hips and shoulders should be parallel to the aim of the clubface.

Remember!

The basic idea of the golf grip is that you should hold the club at address in the same way as you intend to apply it to the ball at impact.

Let the aim of the clubface position the ball relative to the feet

The important and often neglected matter of ball positioning in relation to the feet is greatly simplified by correct clubface aiming. Step up from behind the ball looking down your target line and set the clubface behind the ball. Looking squarely at your target you will notice that, by positioning the face of the club in this way, you also establish a particular alignment of its shaft, and thus also of its handle. It is important when positioning the clubface that the loft is maintained.

Now, without changing that shaft and handle alignment, finalize your grip on the club and shuffle your feet into what feels like the best position to enable you hit the ball straight to your target.

'Stand to the club' correctly in this manner and you will find that the ball is automatically positioned correctly in relation to your feet with every club in the bag, including even the putter.

Too simple? Well, give it a try. Particularly if you're one of the many golfers who habitually position their feet before they aim the clubface, you'll be delighted with the results.

21

Check your posture

Correct posture promotes a body pivot that swings the club on the proper in-to-in arc and in the proper plane, which is the only way to return the clubface to the ball squarely and at the correct angle of attack while completely releasing the clubhead.

In the perfect posture (centre) your weight
is evenly balanced.

Grip the club, aim its face, align your body and position the ball correctly and you will automatically achieve most of the postural requirements of a fine set-up. Just to be sure, though, here are the important areas to check:

- To make room for your arms to swing freely past your body, you must lean over to the ball. Do so from your hips, keeping your back as straight as you comfortably can.

22

- Think of 'head up' rather than 'head down' and achieve it by keeping your chin high.
- Let your arms hang easily straight down from your shoulders, keeping your left arm straight but not stiff and your right arm relaxed at the elbow.
- Because your right hand is lower on the club than your left, your shoulders will tilt slightly to the right, which will encourage positioning of your head behind the ball. Go with the tendency, but don't exaggerate it.
- Stay well balanced and 'springy' by setting your weight equally between the balls of both feet, with your knees slightly flexed.

Short or tall

Your precise posture at address will be influenced by your build. Tall golfers, of necessity, stand relatively close to the ball and thus fairly upright. Short golfers must stand farther away from the ball, and thus lean forward more from the waist. Seek comfort and good balance by avoiding extremes.

A soft right arm

At address, keep your right arm 'soft' and let it bend a bit at the elbow, which will point to your right hip.

Jack's pre-shot routine helps sharpen focus

I think Jack Nicklaus summed up brilliantly the value of a pre-shot routine when he said: 'Give your imagination free rein when you're in a position to win and it can be the death of you.'

He is referring to the fact that if you let your mind wander, especially into the future, you're in big trouble. A pre-shot routine stops this happening. It crystallizes your thoughts and helps you focus the mind on the things that are relevant, to the exclusion of everything else.

My advice to you is develop a consistent pre-shot routine. It doesn't need to be exactly the same as Jack's, but I think it should incorporate certain elements from the great man.

Firstly, picture the shot in your mind's eye, from behind the line of play. This gets you mentally 'into your shot', so you're thinking positively and constructively. Next, aim the clubhead over an intermediate target, a few feet in front of you between the ball and the flag. It's far easier than aiming at a flag 250 yards away. Also, be very specific about what you aim at. This is relatively easy when the flag is your target. But when you're driving off the tee, perhaps not so easy. Never aim just anywhere down the middle, because in my view if you aim vaguely you swing vaguely too – and that's when you're prone to making stupid mistakes.

Work hard at perfecting your pre-shot routine when you're at the driving range. This is the place where you develop the good habits that enable you to perform to a higher level in competition. Nobody ever practised as well as Jack did. In my opinion, amateur golfers hit too many shots on the range with too little thought. Try to get into the mindset of hitting fewer balls with more thought. Quality, not quantity – that's what practising is all about.

*The ideal pre-shot routine: Visualise the shot, then aim the
clubface, and finally build your stance.*

The golf swing's only purpose

The majority of the world's 35 million golfers never play
the game as well as they could because they have no idea,
an incorrect idea, or an incomplete idea of what they are
trying to do when they swing a golf club.

The golf swing has only one purpose: to deliver the head
of the club to the ball correctly.

How that is done is immaterial, so long as the method
permits correct impact to be achieved over and over and
over again.

Golf's only secret

The behaviour of the golf ball is determined solely by four impact factors interacting with each other. They are:

1. The direction in which the face of the club looks, or the *clubface alignment*.
2. The direction in which the clubhead travels, or the *path of the swing*.
3. The angle of inclination at which the clubhead arrives at the ball, or the *angle of attack*.
4. The *speed* of the clubhead.

Everything you do in swinging a golf club should be related to these all-important impact factors. Getting them right is golf's only secret

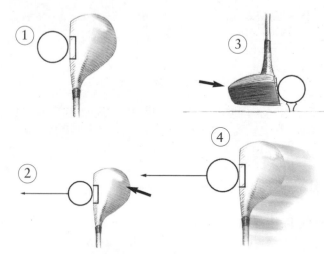

Golf's four key impact factors determine the shape and quality of your shots.

The flight of the ball tells all

The behaviour of every golf shot is determined not by how the club is swung – by the form of bodily motions employed – but by how each swing delivers the clubface to the ball. However, everything is moving too fast for the golfer to see what is happening on impact. How, then, can he discover the alignment of the clubface, the path of the swing, the angle of attack, and the speed of the clubhead?

The answer is: the flight of the ball.

The single most important step in becoming a good golfer: knowing what you should be trying to do with the club by learning and accepting the game's true fundamentals – the correct 'geometry' of impact.

The next most important step is acquiring the knowledge that enables you to identify what's happening at impact from the flight of your shots. Master those two mental disciplines and your eventual playing ability becomes solely a matter of how hard you are willing and able to work at golf. The 'geometry' of golf is set out in the following pages as clearly as I know how. If you gain nothing else from this book, learn it well and use it wisely.

When the clubhead swings from out to in

THE SLICE: ball starts left of target line then curves right.
- The swing path is from out to in across the target line.
- The clubface looks to the right of, or is open to, the swing path, resulting in an oblique or 'cutting' impact with the ball that creates clockwise sidespin.

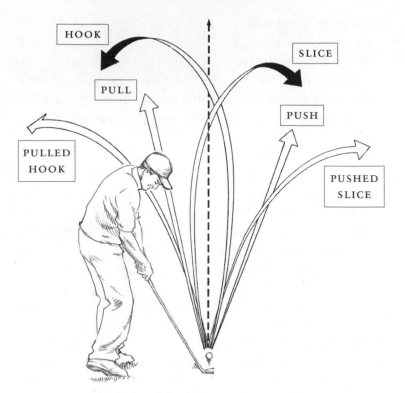

HOOK

SLICE

PULL

PUSH

PULLED
HOOK

PUSHED
SLICE

*The flight of the ball reveals everything
about your swing.*

- As the ball's forward momentum decreases, the clock-wise sidespin curves the ball more and more to the right.
- The more open the clubface and/or the more out to in the swing path, the stronger the sidespin and the more pronounced the slice.
- Also, the more out to in the clubhead path, the steeper the angle of attack, thus the more oblique the impact in a perpendicular as well as horizontal plane.
- The combination of clockwise sidespin and additional

backspin produced by the open clubface and/or the steep angle of attack makes this the weakest shot in golf, flying excessively high if the ball is contacted at the bottom of the arc, or excessively low if the bottom of the arc is sufficiently forward for the ball to be thinned or topped.

THE PULL: ball flies straight but left of target.
- The swing path is from out-to-in across the target line.
- The clubface is square to the swing path, but closed to the target line.
- Because the clubhead path and clubface alignment 'match', the impact is flush rather than oblique. Thus good distance is obtained.

THE PULLED HOOK: ball starts left of target line and then curves more left.
- The swing path is from out-to-in across the target line.
- The clubface looks to the left of, or is closed to, the swing path resulting in oblique impact with the ball that curves it even more in its starting direction, i.e., to the left.
- At its worst, this shot is literally 'smothered' to the extent that the ball fails to rise sufficiently off the ground to go any appreciable distance.

When the clubhead swings from in to out

THE PUSH: ball flies straight but right of target.
- The swing path is from in-to-out across the target line.
- The clubface is square to the swing path, but open to the target line.

- Because the clubhead path and clubface alignment match, the impact is flush rather than oblique and good distance is obtained.

THE HOOK: ball starts right of target then curves left
- The swing path is from in-to-out across the target line.
- The clubface looks to the left of, or is closed to, the swing path resulting in an oblique contact with the ball that creates anticlockwise sidespin.
- As the ball's forward momentum decreases, the anticlockwise sidespin curves the ball more and more to the left.
- The more closed the clubface and/or the more in to out the swing path, the stronger the sidespin and the more pronounced the hook.
- Also, the more in-to-out the clubhead path, the shallower the angle of attack, thus the greater the risk of the clubhead catching the ground before the ball, resulting in either fat or thin contact.
- Assuming clean back-of-the-ball impact, the combination of lower flight and additional roll resulting from a slightly closed clubface and slightly in to out clubhead path – i.e., a draw as opposed to a full-blooded hook – produces more distance for a given amount of clubhead speed than any other impact configuration.

THE PUSHED SLICE: ball starts right of target then curves more right.
- The swing path is from in-to-out across the target line.
- The clubface looks to the right of, or is open to, the swing path resulting in oblique impact with the ball that

curves it even further in its starting direction, i.e., to the right.

- The type of in-to-out swing path necessary to produce this impact geometry invariably results in reduced clubhead speed and, therefore, poor distance.
- It should be noted, as an aside, that today's excessive fear of swinging 'over the top' makes this type of shot very common at most levels of the game. The cure lies in allowing the clubface to square automatically at impact by swinging the clubhead through the ball from in-to-in, relative to the target line.

When the clubhead swings on target

THE STRAIGHT SHOT: ball starts and continues on target line.
- The swing path at impact matches or exactly coincides with the target line.
- The clubface looks squarely or directly at the target.
- Because the clubhead path and the clubface alignment 'match' perfectly, i.e., there is no obliqueness, the impact is flush and the trajectory is correct, resulting in optimum carry and roll for the amount of clubhead speed delivered to the ball.

THE FADE: ball starts slightly left of the target line then curves back to target towards end of flight.
- The clubhead path at impact is slightly across the target line from out to in.
- The clubface looks squarely at, or very slightly to the right of, the target. This slight mismatching or obliqueness of clubhead path and clubface alignment produces

just enough clockwise sidespin to drift the ball to the right, while delivering the clubhead at a sufficiently shallow angle for the blow to be forcefully forward rather than weakly downward or upward, as in the slice.

- Extra height and fast stopping, for relatively little distance loss, make the fade a popular shot among stronger tournament-level golfers.

THE DRAW: ball starts slightly right of target line then curves back to target towards end of flight.

- The clubhead path at impact is slightly across the target line from in to out.
- The clubface looks squarely at or very slightly to the left of the target.
- The slight mismatching or obliqueness of clubhead path and clubface alignment produces just enough anti-clockwise sidespin to drift the ball gently to the left late in its flight, as the strong forward momentum resulting from the shallow angle of clubhead delivery diminishes.
- The lower flight and additional roll resulting from the slightly closed clubface make this the shot of choice for the majority of the world's golfers. Indeed, repeatedly producing the impact geometry that draws the ball creates all the best set-up and swing habits and mechanics, from which players can then much more easily learn to play all the other 'shapes' of shot.

Why knowing golf's geometry is so important

Being able to identify the 'geometry' of impact from the flight of the ball is fundamental to playing golf up to your maximum potential. Given that ability, everything you do in learning, building and maintaining a golf swing is directed towards achieving the game's number one fundamental: correct impact. Without that ability, each swing lacks focus; occurs in a vacuum; is little more than a hit-and-hope experiment.

Once you completely understand the 'geometry' of the game, all you have to do to analyse your swing – to decide how to correct it or improve it – is to think about the way the golf ball reacts when you hit it. And because that exercise is purely a mental one, you can do it anywhere: sitting at home, even, as well as on the golf course or driving range.

Pupils are amazed that, once they have described their basic shot patterns to me, I can give them a lesson over the telephone. The reason is that the flight of the ball tells me everything I need to know, both to diagnose their swing faults and to formulate the cure.

The flight of your shots will provide you with that information also, if only you will let it. And letting it will make golf a much easier game than you ever believed possible.

Square your body to the clubface

Because they can see their foot alignment but not how their upper bodies are aimed at address, many golfers find it easy to stand square but hard to align their shoulders parallel to the target line consistently. One way to check your body alignment is by 'reading' the first part of the ball's flight when you hit practice shots, before sidespin affects its direction. Given solid understanding of golf's impact 'geometry', shots consistently starting left tell you that you are probably aligned too much that way, or are too 'open' at address. Conversely, shots starting right indicate that you are aligned too far right, or are too 'closed', at address.

Aim the gun

Study the top professionals and you will see them constantly working with teachers or friends on their address angles. The reason is, of course, that a gun aimed incorrectly never hits the target.

Pattern your grip thus . . .

Exactly how the club nestles into your palm and fingers will depend on the size and flexibility of your hands. Seek a hold with the left hand in which your last three fingers can press the club firmly, but not rigidly, against the fleshy pad below your thumb. Every time you take your grip, remember that you must relate your hands to your target through the clubface.

The club will naturally sit a little more in the fingers of your right hand than it does in your left, and you will probably secure the club most comfortably by holding it firmly, but not tightly, with your two middle fingers. 'Wrap' your right hand snugly against your left, so that the pad below your right thumb caresses the top of your left thumb. By more-or-less matching the direction of the Vs formed by your thumbs and forefingers, you set your hands parallel to each other, which encourages them to work as a unit during the swing.

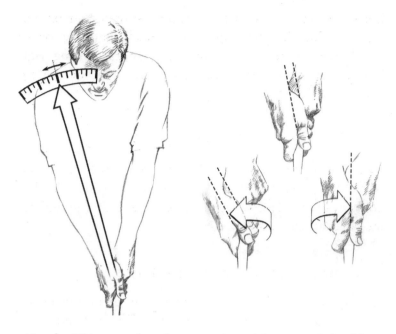

*Aim the 'Vs' somewhere between your right eye and shoulder,
experimenting to see what works best for you.*

. . . but experiment between these extremes to discover what works for you

The correct grip for you is the one that delivers your
clubface square to your direction of swing during impact.
The grip pattern that does that for Jack Nicklaus or Lee
Trevino may not do it for you, so face up to the need
for some experiment. This will probably be uncomfortable
at first, but if you skip it you can forget ever becoming
a good golfer, because your repeated misalignment of the
clubface at impact will consistently create faults in your
set-up and swing.

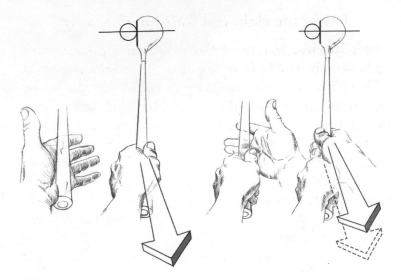

*Take great care in forming your grip,
so that it is repeatable.*

Start with your Vs pointing midway between your nose and your right shoulder. If the flight of your shots tells you that you are delivering the clubface to the ball looking to the right of your swing line, move both your hands gradually towards a strong position – i.e., so the Vs point more away from your nose and to the outside of your right shoulder. If your shots tell you that the clubface is arriving at the ball looking left of your swing path, move both your hands gradually towards a weak position – i.e., so the Vs point more at your nose.

Your grip is right for you when your shots fly straight, even though you may be pulling the ball left or pushing the ball right of target. No curve on your shots shows that your clubface alignment and swing direction are matched.

Hover the clubhead for a smooth start

One distinctive feature of Greg Norman's game is how he hovers the clubhead of his driver above the ground at address. It's one of the things that he picked up as a young man from a Jack Nicklaus instruction book. Greg claims that it keeps tension out of his hands and arms, which promotes a smooth, wide one-piece takeaway and good overall rhythm in his swing. That makes sense. He also says it enables him to maintain a constant grip pressure, removing the tendency to re-grip the club at address. Again, sound advice, since a lot of club golfers have a habit of re-gripping which not only results in grip flaws, but also upsets the clubface alignment before the swing has even started.

I think hovering the clubhead at address has another very important benefit. It encourages you to stand a little bit taller at address, rather than hunch over the ball, and that improvement in your posture helps promote a better turn.

Simply Peter

With his appointment as the professional at Sandy Lodge, I would sometimes practise with Peter Thomson. This was in the 1950s, when the Australian was picking up one Open Championship after another. He once went out to Sandy Lodge specifically to get me to look at his set-up – just that, his set up to the ball, nothing else. Satisfied that he was standing well to the ball, he then drove back into the centre of London. I draw an important lesson from this: '70 per cent of all the bad shots which are hit are due to a faulty set up to the ball.'

Back to basics refresher

The grip controls where the clubface looks at impact, which determines the final direction or curvature of the shot through its interaction with the path of the clubhead.

The alignment of the body relative to the target line largely controls the direction in which the clubhead is swung through the ball, which determines the starting direction of the shot – *and, if there is no curvature*, also its final direction.

If you've watched professionals on the practice tee at tournaments, you may have wondered why they spend so much time and effort checking their alignments at address – more in many cases, than working on actual swing moves. The above is the answer. Good golfers are good golfers largely because they have learned and accepted that, no matter how fine the gun's firing action, unless it is aimed correctly it won't deliver the missile to the target. Lesser golfers are so impatient to pull the trigger, or so wrapped up in the mechanics of the swing, they never master what comes before.

CHAPTER 2

Building a Better Golf Swing

How to start back 'square'

A lot of rubbish has been talked and written about the way a golfer should swing the club back from the ball. There have been those who advocated rolling the wrists, those who advocated holding the clubface 'square' as long as possible, and those who swore by hooding the clubface during the takeaway.

The 'squares' are the ones on the ball, but the trouble is that they don't always define what is truly 'square'. The golf swing combines an arc and a plane. How, then, do you get 'square'?

The answer is by swinging the club away from the ball in one coordinated movement – without any *independent* action of any part of the body, especially the hands and arms.

Prove it for yourself as follows. Take your aim and set up correctly for a full shot. Now, without rotating your hands and arms or consciously cocking your wrists, but making the club as near as possible an extension of your left arm, turn and tilt your shoulders slightly and let your arms swing back in concert with this movement. The club will have moved back *inside* the target line – there is no other place it can go if you have set-up and turned properly. And the clubface – where will it point? Not at the sky – which would have happened if you had rolled your wrists clockwise. Not at the ground – which would have happened if you'd held the face down or hooded. It will be pointing more or less *forward* – at right angles to the arc of your swing.

This is 'square', as you can very quickly prove by turning your shoulders back to their original position, when the clubface will return squarely behind the ball.

And that is the correct takeaway.

Turn your body, cock the wrists

I had played golf from childhood – and had a club in my hand from the time I could stand up. I suppose, at 15 or 16, I could get round Lindrick on occasions in under 70, but at other times I would have to walk in from the course because I had run out of golf balls. I was gifted in the sense of being able to hit the ball because I had grown up with it and had the chance of watching fine players in the area – Arthur Lees, Frank Jowle, Johnny Fallon and, of course, my cousin Jack. So when Willie Wallis (my boss and the head professional at the Hallamshire where I got my first job as assistant) said to me: 'You must turn your body and use your lumbar muscles and you must cock the wrists,' I took notice of it.

Today I will tell pupils they must turn the body because you have to do that to get the clubhead swinging from inside to inside, and you must cock the wrists otherwise the club will follow the body too much. What Willie was saying was similar to what I am saying today. The difference is that I explain it, whereas he didn't.

Keeping it simple

You are now taking great care to pre-programme, as far as possible, correct impact through your grip, clubface aim, ball position, and body alignment and posture. All that remains for you to play the best golf of which you are capable is to swing the club on a plane and in a direction that transmits your address 'geometry' to the ball, while also generating sufficient clubhead speed to propel it the required distance.

How do you do that?

Because the ball is lying on the ground to the side of you, the answer is with an upward and downward swinging of the arms combined with a rotational motion of the body.

How much swinging relative to how much body motion? How 'steeply' up and down should your arms swing relative to the 'aroundness' of your body motion? Which drives what – the arm swinging the body rotation, or the body rotation the arm swinging? Where does the power come from – the swinging motion of the arms or the rotating of the body?

All of those questions, and all others like it, will quickly become moot if you will simply do as follows:

Swing your left arm directly back from the ball, allowing it to move progressively upward and backward – i.e., to the inside of the target line – as a natural response to the rotation of your shoulders around the axis of your spine.

Can the golf swing really be that simple?

Well, if you ever reach the point of feeling that your chief golfing problem has become 'paralysis by analysis', forgetting everything but the above concept of backswing motion might delightfully surprise you.

Wind up – don't lift up

When teaching, I get pupils to finish the backswing completely, before starting the downswing, by asking them to point the clubhead consciously at the target before starting down. This virtually ensures a full shoulder pivot and a complete wrist cock.

Under and out of the way

I have often asked myself what is common to all good strikers of a golf ball. The only thing I can find which they all seem to do is that they hit *under*. By that, I mean that the right side relaxes and swings under a taller left side through the ball. This means that in the hitting area the shoulders are tilted, and yet the left hip is turned to some extent towards the target so as to get the body out of the way sufficiently to allow the hands and arms room to hit through.

Let me now try to define the downswing. To allow the right side to swing under, the first thing to do in the downswing is to move the hips laterally to the left. This can only be achieved by good leg action. This is the *under* part of the swing. The start down with the lower half of the body will have brought the hands and arms down to hip height, leaving the shoulders behind.

From here we concentrate on the *out of the way* part as

we cut loose with the hands and arms. The head, I hardly need to say, must remain still during all of this. Indeed, if there is a secret to hitting under and past the body it is to keep the head behind the ball until the ball is in its way.

The classic golf swing requires little more than 'two turns and a swish'. Note the spine angle remains constant.

Don't be a statue!

Are we not getting far too position-conscious and forgetting the all-important thing – to swing the club?

We have had in the recent past a spate of golf books, full of positions that dissect the golf swing. It is important to remember that the players shown in this way *swing through* the positions you see in the books, and I suppose never really feel the different positions you see when looking at the pictures.

All too frequently we see potentially great golfers putting themselves into that late hitting position of a Hogan and a Snead (or today, an Els or a Woods). This sort of thing is of no value whatsoever! In fact, I would say it is harmful, in that anyone who tries to *put* himself into this position has so obviously missed the reason why the great players are able to swing this way.

The wrists are *not* consciously held back in the downswing until the last moment. This really is too difficult to do. Learn to swing and swing correctly, and the wrists will uncock at the right time. I get the impression that many of our young players are making a conscious effort not to let the clubhead work in the hitting area. In other words, they are so keen on late hitting that they are never actually using the clubhead at all – despite the fact that hitting is surely the most natural thing to do with the clubhead, certainly more natural than trying to hold the clubhead back!

Grip, stance and pivot should allow for the hand and wrist action to be absolutely natural, and not forced in any way. If you feel you have to consciously hold the clubhead back, *then there is something wrong* and you are certainly not swinging.

In the past we have seen many unorthodox *swingers* playing great golf. The very fact that they have been swinging has helped them in the groove. I feel sure these players have never become too much bogged down by position. If you are in a wrong position, then certainly try to *swing* through a better one. But whatever you do, don't try to *put* yourself into a better position.

A golfer's waggle usually gives the show away, proclaiming whether he is a swinger or not. The non-swinger is so stilted that we know he is going to go from one position to the next, and never swing the club at all.

The top of the backswing and halfway down positions seem to be the most sought after. How often do we see a player admiring that late-hitting, halfway down position he has put himself into! He can feel where he *should* be. I venture to say that the finest players never feel this position; they feel a much more complete thing, that of swinging the clubhead through the ball to the target. We all freely discuss our golf swings but how many of us have *swings*, or have we just a set of many positions?

Timing – the elusive quality

Most modern books on golf have abundant and arresting action pictures, showing positions in the backswing, down-swing, and followthrough. Perhaps it is this factor, as much as any other, which causes us to think of a swing in three distinct parts. To do that may be well enough, except that sometimes it can lead to the loss of that essential element in our swing known as timing.

What an elusive word that is in relation to the golf swing! One hears, so often, 'my timing was a little bit off today' when some unfortunate has had a bad day, and, as it happens to so many of us, it is perhaps not a bad thing if we try to be more specific and pinpoint this gremlin of bad timing, which can strike at the best of swings.

When it happens to me, I try to remember one thing, and often it helps; it is this: 'Remember, I want my maximum speed at impact – not before'.

If I can let this really penetrate my mind, it is the easiest way to cut out that quick snatch back from the ball, or the snatch from the top. When I see it in pupils, I find myself saying: 'don't forget it is the ball you are hitting, not the backswing.' Put another way round, what I could say is: 'wait for it', but I think it is easier to wait for it if you know what you are waiting for!

Distance is clubhead speed correctly applied

Let me remind you that 'correctly applied' means:

- Clubface square to target at impact
- Clubhead path momentarily coinciding with target line at impact
- Angle of attack appropriate to club being used at impact.

Never forget that no matter how high your clubhead speed, the greater the error in any one of those angles, the less useful distance you will gain.

Straight enough

The left arm is the radius of the swing arc and it must maintain that radius. To do this it need not be ramrod straight, in the sense that Harry Vardon meant when he said he loved playing against opponents with straight left arms. It must be straight enough, without being stiff. In any case, even if the left arm is slightly bent, it will be straightened out in the hitting area by centrifugal force.

Hitting straight

The beginner, and he who aims to improve his game, must have faith here. He must believe something quite simple; that there is no need to do any conscious squaring of the blade in the downswing, or in the hitting area, with the hands. The hands should be left free for hitting the ball. The correct downswing action from the top, in the correct sequence, will take care of the blade of the club as it swings through the ball.

It really does all depend upon how the body is wound up and unwound. The hands and arms need to swing freely from the hub of the wind-up. Wind-up, then unwind, and swing the clubhead while you are doing this by a free use of the hands and arms. This type of action works for every club in the bag, allowing the loft on each to do the work as necessary.

The right elbow

Ninety-nine percent of floating right elbows – the ones that stick up or out like a chicken's wing – are caused by an incorrect pivot. If you *tilt* your shoulders instead of partly *turning* them, and take your hands back ahead of the clubhead, then you will get a floating right elbow.

Controlling the elbow won't necessarily put the thing right, since it is caused by a combination of pivot and of wrist action following the pivot, which leaves the clubhead behind in the backswing. You cannot correct it by getting the clubhead on its way back first, so that it leads the elbow into the right position, which then feels strong while you turn.

47

You could, of course, hit good golf shots with a floating right elbow, as long as the elbow gets into the right place to hit the ball. But only a right relationship between hands and body can put you into the right position in the easiest way.

When teaching people, there is quite a simple general rule I follow: in both cases, floating right elbow and too-tight elbow, I use what sounds like a local independent variation merely to wipe another one out, in its effect when the player tries to do it. You tend to get a floating right elbow if you leave the clubhead behind your hands. If you then try to start back clubhead first, you often cure it.

Other things being equal, of course, faults can come from both variations. If I drag the clubhead back, that's when I float it; if I start the clubhead back too much ahead, I go flat.

If you don't get the clubhead moving on the way back, then you can't get back to the top of the swing without moving the right elbow out from the body; and the delayed clubhead thus nearly always leads you to a steep position. You can easily spend five minutes explaining this to a player; and he can easily follow this and see how it all works.

There are actually thousands of people with this sort of trouble, because those who have read about and studied the game have been told so much to 'take the club back in one piece'. Trying to do just this, if it is misunderstood, can lead the player straight into a floating right elbow!

With this particular fault, as with so many others in golf, we come back to just one basic thing. May I repeat myself once more and say it again: The relationship between your clubhead, your hands and your body is vital. *If you get the right relationship between your clubhead, your hands and your body, you will never get a floating right elbow.*

Don't forget your hands

Nick Faldo's swing changes in the 1980s centred around a few key elements. He widened his stance so that his legs would stabilize and support a more rotary body action. He then focused on winding his body over a more passive leg and hip action, which created resistance – in effect, energy – that he would then use to drive a more powerful downswing. The arms swung in response to the body motion, whereas in his swing of old the hands and arms dominated the action and the body just went along for the ride. Basically, Nick went from being a very handsy player to a more body-controlled, passive-hands player.

That was just the ticket for Nick, but overemphasis on body action is dangerous territory for the average golfer because it assumes you have a great hand action and, to be frank, most club golfers suffer from a lack of hand action rather than too much. That's why I often prefer to use the arc of the swing to get the body moving. Once you get the correct in to in picture of the swing path, your body will clear out of the way virtually automatically, creating the proper release of the hands and thus the clubhead through the ball.

You 'aim' the clubhead at the top as well as at address

If your clubshaft parallels your target line at the top of the backswing, the club is ideally 'aimed' to swing back through the ball along the target line.

If your shaft is angled left of the target line at the top, there will be a tendency to swing the clubhead across the line from out-to-in and either slice or pull the shot. Conversely, if the shaft is angled right of the target line at the top, there will be a tendency to swing the clubhead from in to out across the target line and either hook or push the shot.

Understanding swing plane . . . in simple terms!

The plane on which you swing is established chiefly by your address position. As you stand to the ball comfortably and squarely, neither cramped nor reaching, your left arm and the club form a more-or-less continuous straight line. The angle of that line, relative to the vertical, is the ideal plane on which to swing the club up and down with your arms.

What you are aiming to do, in golfing terms, is to shift your right side out of the way in the backswing and your left side out of the way in the throughswing, so that at the moment of impact the club is being swung freely by your arms with the clubhead moving straight through the ball, along the target line.

More about swing plane!

Numerous enlightening books and articles appear describing varying aspects of the golf swing. But there are some aspects that rarely find their way into print. Plane, for example. I intend here to single it out for the special attention it merits, if rarely attains. Why is plane so important? Because if the plane of your swing is correct, the angle of attack on the ball is correct. That sounds difficult. Let's look closer.

Generally speaking, a swing in the correct plane gives you a *fairly flat bottom to the swing*, which is what we want in order that the power we are unleashing will proceed directly through the ball. The same amount of power, or more power, applied more steeply or from an incorrect plane, cannot hope to hit the ball so far.

My idea of a correct plane is one in which if, at the top of the backswing, we extend the line from the left hand to the left shoulder downwards, that line should then approximately aim at the ball.

It is obvious, then, that the plane of the swing will vary with the distance one is standing from the ball. This in turn varies with whatever club we are playing. For example, one stands close with a 9-iron, because of its short shaft; and the resulting swing is much more upright than the swing with a driver.

There is no real problem with this change of plane, though; for from the player's angle it is purely automatic and should merely vary directly with the length of club used.

Now, in the correct pivot in the backswing there is a certain degree of shoulder *turn*, linked with a certain degree of shoulder *tilt*. One can soon deduce how a swing with too little downward tilt of the left shoulder, and too much turn, will be too flat. Similarly, one with too much tilt, and not enough turn, becomes too upright.

Each swing, though, produces its own characteristics. A 'too upright' arc usually makes for better iron play than wooden club play, since these iron shots are hit on the downswing. Correspondingly, a 'too flat' swing often works very well with the woods, but is of little value for iron shots, since these are then hit nearer the bottom of the arc.

The present vogue is to aim at an upright swing – which I suppose I would prefer to a flat one. But why not swing *in plane* – which will then be the right degree of uprightness for all shots?

Don't spin your shoulders

If you spin your shoulders too early in the downswing, it throws the club outside the ideal swing path which means you're right on track for a pull or slice. This is perhaps the most common fault I see at club golfer level.

If that sounds familiar, think about how you swing your hands and arms down from the top. I'm reminded of the great Harry Vardon, six time Open champion, who said that as he changed direction from backswing to down-swing, he felt his hands swung down to hip height before his body even began to unwind. In reality, he combined the perfect arm swing with the ideal body rotation, but his feeling was one of swinging the arms down first and this is a swing that that would definitely help you if you slice. It encourages the hands and arms to play a more dominant role, swinging the club down into impact on the ideal path and plane.

Don't let tuition destroy your natural rhythm

As a teacher I'm forever conscious of the fact that tuition must never get in the way of the natural rhythm in a golfer's swing. I remember teaching Seve at Wentworth in 1979 and thinking: 'I've got to be careful here.' He had such wonderful rhythm that I didn't want to tell him anything about his swing that might upset it. So all of my advice to him was in consideration of that fact.

When Seve was playing well there wasn't an ounce of tension in his body. I believe that some of the problems in the 1990s stemmed from the fact that he'd become perhaps overly concerned with techniques and swing thoughts, which has never quite been his style, and thus taken away some of that natural softness and impeded the free-flowing motion of his swing.

This is a danger for any golfer. Whenever you get taught something new, the first instinct is to tighten-up and that process usually starts with the grip. You must be aware of this and avoid tension creeping into your hands. Never lose the gift of being able to swing the club freely. Keeping your grip soft will almost certainly help. As Peter Thomson used to say: 'Always grip lightly because you'll instinctively firm up at impact anyway.' That's not a bad philosophy to bear in mind whenever you're trying to make changes to your swing.

If you wind yourself like a spring . . .

I like to compare body action in the golf swing to the winding and unwinding of a spring. Think of it this way and you will realize how important it is that the bottom half of the spring should resist the turning of the top half, in order to increase coiling (and thereby power).

The feeling should be one of staying relatively still, but 'lively', from the waist down, while your torso turns around the axis of your spine and your arms and hands swing the club back and up so that it ultimately points parallel to the target line. The left leg will give a little, turning in towards the right, and the left heel will usually be pulled rather than lifted off the ground. But the effort should be to prevent, rather than encourage, such movements – *while making sure your shoulders turn as your arms swing the club back and up.*

. . . automatically you will let it all fly

Create sufficient torque with your upper-body backswing wind-up and you cannot help but release it into a powerful throughswing. As your legs and hips win the battle of the opposing forces, and pull spring-like towards the target, swing your arms straight down before your shoulders spin. Never do anything to inhibit a free arm-swing.

Keep your head down? Forget it!

When I was on the instruction panel of the American magazine *Golf Digest* in the 1960s they carried out a survey of the leading 50 money winners on tour. They photographed each golfer hitting shots, with a grid pattern positioned behind them so it was possible to monitor their head movement during the swing. Of these, 48 of the 50 golfers moved their head to the right in the backswing. Some moved more than others and two golfers remained centred. But, not surprisingly since these were all good players, none moved to the left.

The obsession among some club golfers to keep the head down has kept me busy for 50 years. It's like strapping a straightjacket on to a golfer; it restricts a full, free turn, so essential for both power and accuracy.

So if ever I hear of a golfer whose main swing thought is to keep their head down throughout the swing, the alarm bells ring in my head. In any good swing there is invariably a certain amount of lateral movement of the head and body. So long as this body action is harmonized with the hand and arm action, it is allowable and in many cases desirable for there to be a degree of lateral movement.

Careful of some other clichés

Let's punch holes in a few more of some prime 'book' clichés:

'Go back slowly': This is nothing short of an invitation to disaster. It leads to moving rather than swinging the club back, in a motion completely lacking in rhythm. If you go back at the pace that the slow-back proponents suggest, you have got to control the club every inch of the way, which, apart from anything else, is too much of a mental exercise.

What you should do instead is set the swing off

smoothly at a pace that will enable you to come down quicker than you go up. I find most players swing at the correct pace when they remember they want their maximum speed at impact.

'Tuck in the right elbow': A right elbow flying away from the body is usually caused by a steep tilt of the shoulders in the backswing, rather than a combined tilt-turn. It is equally wrong, however, to suggest – as some teachers still do – placing a handkerchief between the right elbow and the body and keeping it there in the backswing and downswing. The right elbow will find its correct position if the shoulder turn and the arm swing are correct.

'Follow through': Making a conscious effort to follow through nicely when the rest of the swing is thoroughly bad leads to nothing but confusion and frustration. The initiation of the downswing completely commits you all the way to and *through* the followthrough. So, if you think your followthrough is bad, look for something wrong much earlier – possibly your grip, set-up, backswing or the way you start your downswing. Remember that a correct followthrough is the result of a correct start down.

Sweep those arms down and through

The action of the arms is the most neglected area in golf instruction. There have been 'hands' methods, and 'body' methods, but the fact is that, whatever method he hung his hat on, every good golfer in history has swept the club through the ball fast and freely with his arms.

Words always in season

When I am teaching I continually find myself using some phrases over and over again to player after player. Since these would seem to be the ones I have found most helpful to the most players, it may be worth repeating them yet once more. They are:

1. Don't lift up; wind up.
2. Start the backswing with the right shoulder getting out of the way.
3. Point the clubhead at the target in the backswing. This, incidentally, is a quick way of getting a beginner to pivot, and to cock the wrists.
4. As near as possible, keep your feet flat on the ground.
5. Stay 'sat down' as you turn your shoulders.

How – and what – to practise

I assume that the fact that you are reading this book means you want to improve your golf. I further assume that you want to improve badly enough to be prepared to give some time – even time that you would normally have spent playing – to practising the game. Some of us are 'naturally' more talented golfers than others, but *all* of us need to practise to develop and hold our full potential.

I have spent a lot of time teaching, so I know a fair amount about the habits of the average golfer in terms of their approach to practice. And what has come home to me is that he has a great deal to learn, not simply about the technicalities of golf, but about the sheer mechanics of practising it. What seven out of ten golfers do when they go to a driving range, or down to the club with a bag of balls, may be exercise, but it isn't practice.

Let us start, therefore, by defining practice. It has three distinct forms.

The first and absolute primary form of practice you do at home sitting in an armchair, or driving the car to work. You can do it with your brain, and it consists of thinking through the cause-and-effect of whatever you were doing the last time you played golf. From here, still strictly on the mental plane, you decide through a logical reasoning process, not guesswork, exactly what you will be trying to achieve the next time you practise. Ideally, these thought processes should be based on lessons you have been taking from a professional in whom you have confidence. There is no substitute for personal tuition – for advice tailor-made for you as an individual. The vitally important thing, however, is never to practise until you have a clear picture of what you are trying to do.

The next form of practice is the physical execution of what you have planned mentally. This is swing-building and game-improving practice, and we will look at it in detail in a moment.

The third form of practice, which all good players do, and which I'd like to persuade you to do, is the prelude to any important round of golf. It isn't practice in the previous sense, because you are not trying to rebuild your game (or at least you shouldn't be). What you are trying to do, with anything from 10 to 50 shots, is to tune up the game you possess on that particular day; to loosen muscles, to get the 'feel' of the clubs, to bring the club-face into the ball squarely and solidly and thereby boost your confidence for the ensuing round. And to find one workable swing thought for the day. This is the form of practice few club players bother to make the effort to do, but which is indispensable if you have serious golfing ambitions.

Having defined practice, let us now get back to the actual techniques of its swing-building form. Once you get to the practice ground with cause, effect and treatment all clearly in mind, don't worry too much about where you hit the balls – especially if you are making a major swing change. Your fault will have been grooved, and the action incorporating it will probably feel comfortable. The cure might at first feel very strange, but you must persevere if a lasting improvement is to be made. If no improvement can be made over a reasonable period, rethink the problem or go back to your golf teacher.

Next, before you even draw a club from the bag, pick a definite point of aim. It doesn't matter what it is or how far away it is, so long as you can focus upon it easily.

Now, take out not your sand-wedge nor your driver, but your 6-iron. This club represents the mean average between the extremes of loft, shaft-length and power. It is the ideal swing-building club.

With the 6-iron in your hand, the point of aim in your eye, and your swing objectives crystal clear in your mind, 'break down the adhesions' with a few easy – but not careless – shots. Right from the outset try to grip correctly, aim the club as the first step in setting-up and set yourself correctly to that clubface alignment.

As you move into the session, try with every shot – *and I mean every single shot* – to do what your preliminary analysis has told you will give you a more solid strike or a straighter flight. Stick to your guns on this long enough to determine whether your mental assessment and cure was right. If it was, keep on practising it only as long as you have plenty of mental and physical energy and enthusiasm. Then plant the relevant 'feel' firmly in your mind for the next actual game you play.

My method of doing this sort of work – and it is work mentally and physically – would involve basically a 6-iron, a hundred balls and as many one-hour spells a week as I could manage. Even if I were a weekend player, I think I would be prepared to sacrifice actual playing time in order to make a lasting improvement. For instance, if I normally played 12 hours a week, I would play perhaps six and practise the other six.

If your assessment and cure are proved wrong after fair trial, do not give up, start experimenting at random, or lose your temper and pop off balls like a pom-pom gun. Take a rest. Go and sit down somewhere and think it all through sensibly again.

The flight of the ball tells you what you are doing, in your grip, in your swing line relative to the target line, and in the angle at which your club is attacking the ball. *Use* this information at all times. Therein lies the only 'secret' of golf.

A lot of resolution is necessary to carry through this kind of programme, as it is to stick with any change in method when actually playing the course. Until the new system works, rounds played can be less than satisfying (which is a good reason for not playing too many!). If it is essential to try to play well on occasion while in the middle of changing your swing, obviously a compromise will have to be made.

I know only too well that weather and golf club

facilities in Britain are against consistent and studied practice, but I am equally sure that if a golfer is keen enough he will find a means. As a last resort, he can erect a golf net at home. For years I used to smash golf balls into a net in my garage, and this is very valuable swing-changing practice, first because you haven't got a result to worry about, and secondly because there is no one to see how badly you are hitting the ball. If you are that keen but don't have the facilities to put up a net, try knocking lightweight plastic balls off an old doormat. Anything you can do to build up your golf muscles, to 'groove' good actions, to keep swinging, must eventually pay dividends.

At the very worst, try every day to swing a club at home for a few minutes – concentrating on what you would be doing if you were hitting balls.

One more important point. There is yet another type of practice – the kind one does on the course in preparing for a tournament. Many people go about it wrongly.

Never play more than 27 holes a day in practice, especially the day before an event. It is essential to conserve both energy and enthusiasm for the actual competition. Very few world-class golfers ever play more than one round a day in practice.

Don't play sloppily in practice rounds. Try to hit the ball solidly, and don't be frightened of scoring well. A good practice round builds confidence.

Give yourself time to take note of the course and your own play. You need two or three extra balls handy to play extra shots, especially bunker shots, chips and putts, hitting them from where you think you will have to hit them on the big day. Take particular note of the clubs you play, especially if the weather is fair. In windy or wet conditions, of course, your practice round estimates may have to be revised.

Finally, although you may use your practice rounds to loosen up and make final swing adjustments, never fundamentally change your method during practice rounds. You are stuck with what you've brought with you. Try to make it work as best as possible.

This happens in every good golf swing

Stand facing any good golfer and watch the space between his hands and right shoulder during the downswing. You will see that it widens like lightning. Then watch any golfing friend who slices the ball repeatedly. The space between his hands and right shoulder will not widen as fast, because he swings his body rather than his arms. The speed at which all good golfers widen this angle is proof positive that, although the lower body initiates the downswing, leg and hip action must always be married to a fast, free arm swing.

Baseball analogy helps keep your swing on plane

One last thought, which may ring a bell with one or two readers. I think golf is very akin to baseball – in this way; in baseball a player swings in plane with the flight of the ball as it comes towards him. In golf, all we have to do is swing in plane with however far away we are from the ball, which partly depends on what club we are using. For any shot and any club, the plane most likely to be easiest

In any good golfer's swing, the space between the hands and right shoulder widens 'like lightning' in the downswing.

really is that ranging straight up from the ball just over the shoulders, as you stand to address it for the shot.

Try 'two turns and a swish'

Golfers, I am afraid, sometimes like to make the game more complicated than it actually is. My simple definition of the golfing action is 'Two turns combined with an arm and hand swing'. And I am often accused of over-simplification when I use this phrase.

Well, here's a suggestion for you. If your game isn't what you would like it to be at the moment, and especially if you feel confused and snarled up by theory, play your next three rounds strictly on the basis of 'two turns combined with an arm and hand swing'.

Don't think of the backswing as a set of complicated and separate movements, but simply as the first turn. Think only of moving your right side out of the way as your hands and arms swing the club back and up. Simplify your downswing likewise. Forget all the stuff about head, hips, late hitting, and what-have-you. Simply picture your downswing as the second turn, moving your left side out of the way as your arms and hands swing the club down and through the ball.

If you have a decent grip and set-up, and can keep your head reasonably still and your feet firmly on the ground in the backswing, approaching golf this way could do wonders for your score.

You will very quickly learn that the swing really isn't a complicated movement, and that the 'secret' of golf lies in coordinating the turns with the actual swinging of the club – not in a series of geometrically exact, deliberate placement of the club in certain 'positions'.

Find a way to turn . . . even if it's not exactly like Ernie

Ernie Els achieves a massive upper-body turn without lifting his left heel. The hips don't turn much, either, so together that creates a lot of resistance in the legs – the action of a supple man and a powerful hitter.

Most of you reading this will not be as supple as Ernie, but it's important that you find a way to turn your body, in whatever way is appropriate for you personally. For many, this means making certain compromises, such as lifting the left heel to 'release' the left side and thus make it possible to turn. You won't generate as much resistance in the legs, but it's better to do that than keep your left heel planted which might not give you the flexibility to make a sufficient turn.

On a personal note, currently 80 years of age, I can say from experience that it is necessary to release from the ground in order to complete the full upper body turn.

Starting down

The correct start down begins in the lower half of the body – the legs and the hips. That is why telling people to 'stay sat down' in the backswing, and to 'get the left heel down first' in the downswing, is often good advice; doing so consolidates the anchor point of the feet, and starts the hips swinging back into and through the address position. This automatically begins to pull on the arms and hands and unwind them towards the ball.

Just as the swinging wrist-cock of the backswing *ended* with the actual cocking of the wrists, so the swinging uncock of the downswing *ends* with the uncocking of the wrists, as you unleash the power of your hands into the stroke.

Ball forward produces a knock-on effect

Placing the ball correctly opposite the left heel in your stance is essential for the longer clubs in the bag, especially the driver. It sets your upper body 'behind the ball' at address and helps establish the appropriate tilt in the shoulders – the right noticeably lower than the left.

Correct ball position also promotes good weight transfer and encourages the shoulders to turn into a more powerful position at the top of the backswing. This good work in the backswing enables you to unwind the body correctly in the downswing, providing free passage for the hands and arms to swing the club dynamically through impact on the optimum path for power. And with the ball being ideally placed in the stance, the clubhead meets it on the ideal angle of attack. It all adds up to the perfect recipe for long, straight driving.

Play to your strengths

Throughout the 1990s there were very few better drivers of the ball than Colin Montgomerie. His accuracy off the tee stemmed from an ability to cultivate a particular shape of shot – namely, the fade – and trust that shot implicitly on the golf course. He would aim down the left side and ever-so-slightly fade the ball into the middle of the fairway. This tee shot strategy is a great way of playing, because it eliminates half the danger on a golf course.

Think about someone who aims straight down the middle of the fairway. They have only to stray off line by half the width of the fairway to finish in the rough either side. Now look at Colin's strategy. He aims down the left side and fades the ball. If all goes according to plan, the ball finishes in the middle of the fairway. If the ball flies dead straight, he's in the left half of the fairway. And if he over-cuts it, he's in the right half. His margin for error is twice the width of someone who aims down the middle with no particular shape in mind.

That's called playing to your strengths, something all good players do.

For power and position, turn your shoulders 'flatter' than your arm swing

It is a common misconception, even among good golfers, that the shoulders and arms should move on the same plane in the backswing. Look towards the target from behind any top golfer making a full shot to prove to yourself that this doesn't happen. If the arms are to position the club correctly in the backswing, and swing freely in the throughswing, they must swing *up* as the shoulders turn *around*. Trying to marry your arms to your shoulders introduces too much body action into the shot, at the expense of clubhead speed.

Everything you need to know about legs!

It is widely recognised that good leg action is essential to good golf. Unfortunately, few average players really understand what constitutes good leg action. In fact, there is probably as much confusion about this department of the swing as about any technical aspect of the game.

Most golfers know that they (the legs) must work, so many make a deliberate, conscious effort to get them to do so. This usually leads to trouble. It is, for instance, the main cause of the 'ballet dancing' that is so common a spectacle on golf courses around the world every weekend.

If you study the great players in action, and compare their movements with the swings of your friends, you will find that in most cases the good players, on the backswing, have considerably *less* movement from the waist down than do club golfers, but considerably *more* in the throughswing. This is a direct result of resistance, torque, spring-like coiling. The good player coils in the backswing against the resistance of his feet and legs. The release of this power in the throughswing results in strong, positive movements from the waist down as the spring 'springs'. The poor player fails to supply the necessary resistance in his legs and feet. He dances around in such a way that there can be no build-up of torque, no coiling of the spring, in the backswing. Then, there being nothing to release in the throughswing, he is either stiff and wooden in his legs or collapses completely when he comes to hit the ball.

The golf ball cannot be struck powerfully and accurately with any action other than that comparable to the wind-up and release of a coil spring.

If the golfer will believe this, and work at it, he will soon realize that his feet and legs are a critical part of his anatomy. They are his contact with the ground, his platform, and their task is nothing more nor less than to resist – to anchor the end of the spring to a base during both its coiling and release. If that doesn't happen, the result invariably is that the player swings his body rather than the club at the ball – the old story of applying oneself rather than the clubhead.

I think 'relax' has been one of the most damaging words in golf teaching, in that it has often been applied to the whole of the set-up, rather than to the upper areas of the body, where relaxation can promote freedom of movement. For the majority of players, however, relaxation from the hips down is one of the worst thoughts to have in mind. Freedom of movement of the feet and legs is exactly what *isn't* required.

In saying this, I realize the need for care. There will be those who read into these words a necessity to root themselves to the ground like telegraph poles. What we seek, in terms of leg action, is a happy medium between rooted stiffness and uncontrolled sloppiness. Perhaps the best word to describe this feel is 'liveliness' – a sensation that we are planted firmly on the floor, but that from this base we can generate and control the power in the spring system overhead.

Perhaps I can put across that feeling by reiterating that, in my concept of the good golf swing, it is impossible to hold a top-of-the backswing position for more than a few seconds, *because the sheer muscular strain on the legs and hips of the correct wind-up will force them to unwind after a very brief period.*

It is often said that the golf swing starts on the ground, and there is no denying this (try swinging while sitting in a chair if you want proof). Unfortunately, taking the idea literally, many players tend to initiate the swing with a ground-level movement, generally either by lifting the left heel or collapsing the left knee forwards, or both. They are dead ducks from that moment on.

Foot and leg action is never an initiating movement, but is the result of the initial movements, which are the swing away of the arms and club and the turn or wind-up of the shoulders.

Thus, a feeling of 'liveliness' should always be sought at address. To promote this, for a full swing, your weight should be comfortably balanced between the balls and heels of each foot, but favouring the balls if anything. You should strive for firmness and a sense of balance, but also a feeling that you are ready to take off – a poised sensation similar, perhaps, to that of an athlete preparing to run or jump. Above all, your knees must be flexed and – this is an absolute fundamental – the right knee must remain flexed throughout the swing.

If you address the ball, then make the movement that would be your initial movement in sitting down, you are going a long way to establishing the correct set-up for good foot and leg action. But beware that you don't – as so many do – stand up again on a straightened right leg as you begin to swing.

If you start your swing correctly, your left heel will not shoot up off the ground; you will not spin on your left toe as your whole body wobbles round to the right; your left knee will not cave in; your right knee will not straighten and lock. The correct start to a lively, springy wind-up will begin to affect the left foot and leg some time after the club has gone back – usually as it reaches hip height. Around that stage of the swing your left knee will be dragged, by the sheer torque of the wind-up, in towards your right leg. Your left heel may rise slightly, the amount depending on your build and suppleness. But the chief movement of your left foot will be to roll in towards the right, pulling the weight remaining on your left side on to the inside of your left foot, not onto the toe. Throughout this wind-up action, your right leg will hardly move. Above all, your right knee must not straighten.

It might be as well, while we're on the subject of feet and legs, to say something about weight transference – a highly controversial point in golf teaching. Quite candidly, I believe that much of the talk about weight transference has done a lot of harm to a lot of golfers. As I see it, there should never be a conscious or deliberate effort to transfer weight one way or the other in the golf swing. Doing so – apart from promoting all sorts of dance-like antics – leads to a host of other faults, of which tilting and swaying the entire body are prime examples. If your upper body winds up against the springy resistance of your feet and legs, whatever weight transfer is necessary will occur naturally on your backswing.

The same applies in the downswing. If what has gone before is correct, if your downswing starts with a coordinated hip movement and arm swing, your feet and legs will do their job automatically, and transfer your weight naturally. But if your backswing is wrong, with your left leg releasing and your right leg stiffening, it is virtually impossible for your legs and hips to work correctly on the way down. Instead, your shoulders will be forced to take over in that component and ugliest – of all golfing sights, the collapsing heave.

Rhythm and tempo

Jerking and rushing the club back are among the most common faults that I encounter at every level of golf, short of the very top. Their most common causes are anxiety and confusion regarding swing technique, producing an

71

almost irresistible urge to get the action over with as fast as possible. On the physical level, the great destroyer is excessive muscular tension, particularly when it freezes the player into total immobility at address.

Understanding exactly what you are trying to do when you swing, then consciously trying to do it, conditions your mind to allow you to begin the action at a leisurely pace and with a fluidity of motion.

Remaining slightly in motion in some part of your body throughout your set-up procedure, then initiating the swing with a confidence-building 'trigger', guards your muscles against locking up.

Stay relaxed over the ball by gently easing your legs and shoulders and 'hanging' your arms loosely as you complete your set-up. Watch good players to get a feel for these tiny, but vital tension-fighters.

There are numerous ways to trigger the swing, from Sam Snead's and Jack Nicklaus's famous chin-swivel to Gary Player's pronounced right knee kick-in. Most effective for most people is the forward-press, a slight targetwards inclination of the hands and hips from which the player, so to speak, 'rebounds' into a running start.

Again, study the triggers of good players, experiment to find the one that works best for you, then practise it until it becomes second nature.

Ladies, you can hit it farther!

With very few exceptions, women do not hit the ball as far as they could. Indeed, the long hitter among women is immediately exceptional, and will often come into national and even international prominence as a golfer almost on the strength of this ability alone. Such is not true of men's golf, where achieving distance is much less a problem than controlling it.

It is true, of course, that women do not hit the ball as far as men because they do not have the physical equipment to generate comparable clubhead speed. What the woman player must realize, however, is that distance isn't just clubhead speed – it is *clubhead speed accurately applied*. While maybe limited to the extent she can increase her actual clubhead speed, there is usually a great deal she can do to deliver what she possesses more effectively to the ball. It is, in fact, incorrect application of the club – not lack of strength – that makes so many ladies play what I describe as pat-ball golf.

The same clubhead speed that many women golfers apply down and across the ball, with the clubface open, would hit it a heck of a lot farther if it were applied with the clubhead travelling virtually parallel to the ground and along the target line with the face square.

Where distance is concerned, it is paramount for the club to approach the ball from directly behind, as opposed to from above and behind. To swing the clubhead into the very back of the ball on a shallow arc in the impact zone, a woman must use her arms, wrists and hands earlier in the downswing than does a man. For most women golfers, this means a conscious, deliberate effort to get their arms really going from the top of the backswing. There are two reasons for this: (i) it takes longer for a woman to reach her maximum clubhead speed; and (ii) the clubhead is more likely to approach the ball from directly behind, rather than from above, and thus achieve flush contact.

Effects of 'hitting earlier' are very noticeable in the

swings of top woman golfers, and any player anxious to improve would do well to study them. She will see that a great many good women players come up on their toes during the downswing and remain there until well after impact. The reason for it, of course, is to allow the clubhead to swing squarely into the ball on the shallow-bottomed arc engendered by an earlier hit, without it touching the ground behind the ball.

Another result of hitting earlier among ladies is an absence of 'dinner-plate' divots with the irons. Few women have the muscular strength to hit down and through on a steep arc with an iron. Hitting earlier brings the clubhead into the ball on a flatter trajectory, with less divot – but produces just as effective a shot, so long as the ball isn't 'scooped.'

How does a woman golfer hit 'earlier'?

First, she determines that, for ever more, she will not be content to play pat-ball, but will really try to *swish* the club through the ball as fast as possible. This is the mental hurdle that most women club golfers (and a few of better standard) must first surmount if they are going to improve substantially.

On the physical side, the first major factor for attention is usually the grip. Most women tend to cut the ball and, if this is the case, they must not be frightened of adopting a powerful grip. The left hand particularly should be placed well on top of the shaft, with up to three knuckles showing and the thumb well to the right side of the grip. The shaft should be held firmly in both the palm and the fingers, and there should be a feeling that the club is nestling deep into the hand so that the fingers can really hold on to it (if this isn't possible the grips are too thick). The right hand may need to be a little under the shaft, the 'V' of the thumb and forefinger pointing between the right ear and right shoulder, with the club held snug in the fingers, and the forefinger 'triggered' around the shaft.

The grip should feel firm, yet leave the arms flexible, not tense or rigid. If this is difficult with the overlapping grip, try an interlocking or double-handed grip (ensuring, of course, that your hands are as close together as possible). Some experiment may be necessary, especially if you have tended to hold the club 'weakly' – left hand well to the left and right hand on top. Don't be frightened to make it.

A woman who cuts the ball should never stand to her shots in an 'open' position – with feet, hips and shoulders aimed to the left of the target. A slightly closed shoulder alignment will not only help her to swing the club solidly into the back of the ball, but will encourage an inside-out angle of attack that will produce a touch of distance-generating 'draw'.

A wide arc in the backswing is even more essential to women golfers than it is to men, simply to make room for the bigger arc on the way down that is imperative if they are to get the clubhead really motoring. Indeed, most women sense this need for a wide backswing, but un-fortunately their efforts to achieve it often lead to a loss of control, through excessive body movement or a tendency to sway.

Women find it difficult to coil their bodies; to 'wind the spring' that puts power into a golf shot. In an effort to get the necessary width of arc, they release from the ground, turn their whole torso from the feet, as the initial backswing movement. Women as well as men must learn to keep the head reasonably still to 'anchor' the swing; and to turn the upper body from the hips up, while the feet and legs resist.

I am often taken to task for advising players, men and women, to hit earlier with the clubhead, but it is a fact that only when the swing lacks a correct wind-up does early use of the clubhead lead to trouble. Without lower-body resistance, an early hit means a feeble pass at the ball with only the hands and arms. When the swing is correctly anchored and there is a good wind-up of the upper body, a strong swing down of the arms and clubhead is essential to keep pace with the reflex release and uncoiling of the legs and hips.

Two different games!

Today, in the year 2005, men and women professionals hit the ball further than when much of the content in this book was first written. The reasons being:

i) equipment, the superior nature of today's clubs and balls;

ii) physique, the best players are athletes today;

iii) most important, there are now so many good swingers whose impact is so pure and correct; that's why the ball goes a long way. As I have stressed many times over the years, *distance is clubhead speed correctly applied.*

Therefore the gap has widened between handicap players and tournament players. This was just as I predicted the game would develop in the conclusion of my book *Impact on Golf* with Laddie Lucas in the mid-1980s. I envisaged that golf would become almost two different games – in the sense of being totally disparate between the professional and amateur.

When one looks at the facts, this indisputably is now the case. Handicaps of the average player have not come down in the last twenty years. Nor has the overall quality of play improved, despite improvements in club and ball technology. Yet the professional game has come on leaps and bounds, with a greater proportion of the field hitting the ball better, farther, and more consistently. Indeed, I would go as far to say that in the pro game the gap between the best and the rest is narrower than at any time in the history of the game. In all honesty, I do not see that trend being reversed.

CHAPTER 3

The Short Game

Get the picture

Some tournament professionals use a wedge for all the little shots around the green and play them very well. But I cannot stress too strongly that this is not the way for 99 percent of golfers, including Tour players, to play those little chips and pitch shots which are such valuable stroke savers.

The routine should be first to examine the lie of the ball, then to look at the flagstick, then to visualize the ball landing on the green and rolling up to the hole, and finally to select the club most suitable to turn that image into reality.

Visualize . . . then commit

On any pitch or chip you must have a mental picture of the shot you are attempting, before you can even choose the right club for it. I hear far too many players saying things like: 'I always chip with my 7-iron.' When I hear this, I know they don't picture the flight and run of the shot before they play it.

Many factors, of course, affect what picture one may get of a particular shot: the speed of the green, slopes on the green, wind, conditions of the approach to the green, etc, etc. Once you have worked out the shot, select the club that will do the work most simply; then – let it! If you need a low shot to run, you will obviously select a straight-faced club; and when you need height and stop, a more lofted one.

Once you have the right club it is only a question of hitting through the ball, *letting the loft of the club you have chosen give the height and run necessary for the shot.* The hands should be slightly ahead of the ball at address and impact, so that the bottom of the arc will come just after the ball is struck, thus avoiding any scooping action, with its dangers of a 'fluff' or a 'top'.

These two foozles are often caused by choosing too-straight-faced a club for the shot you want. The player senses that the shot is going to run too much and tries to add height and stop to it by flicking the wrists early in the downswing.

Summing up: first select the right club; then let it do the work. And always commit yourself to a specific line and a spot where you want to land the ball. Commitment is so important in the short game. Doubt is your No.1 enemy.

Cause and effect in chipping and pitching

The chip shot is used around the green when there are no hazards between your ball and the hole. The object is to drop the ball on the edge of the putting surface and let it run the rest of the way to the hole. Club selection is largely governed by the distance the ball must carry through the air before reaching the green, and the amount of green between you and the hole. For example, from a few feet off the putting surface a 5-iron might loft the ball to the edge of the green, from where it would roll to the hole. But from 15 yards out, your ball would roll too far. Thus you'd probably need an 8-iron or an even more lofted club.

The pitch shot is the exact opposite of the chip. You use a 9-iron, pitching-wedge or sand-wedge to hit the ball high through the air so that it lands and stops as quickly as possible. It is the shot to play over hazards, or when the green is wet and holding, or for some reason the amount of roll is difficult to judge.

The major difference between the two shots is that you are trying to minimize backspin with a chip shot and to maximize it with a pitch shot. Under normal conditions the chip shot is the safer of the two, because roll is easier to judge than flight, and easier to control. Also, most golfers find it easier on short shots to make solid contact with a less-lofted club, the extreme example being, of course, a putter.

The first step in getting ready to play either a chip or pitch is the same as for any other golf shot. You aim the clubface correctly, take your proper grip on the club, then place your feet in relation to the clubface. On both chip and pitch shots, it helps to have your weight predominantly on the left leg, and to set your hands ahead of the clubface. Your legs should be comfortably flexed and your body fairly relaxed (but never crouched over the ball). Place your feet fairly close together in a slightly open stance, but keep your shoulders parallel to the target line.

Neither a chip shot nor a short pitch shot requires

conscious body action. All you need is a smooth back-and-through swing with your arms, hands and club – an unrushed, even-paced movement, in which the clubface never passes the hands until the ball has been sent on its way.

In both pitching and chipping, the length of shot is determined largely by the length of your backswing. Too short a backswing will lead you to stab quickly at the ball, but swing the club too far back and you'll tend to slow down before impact. In your mental picture of the shot you will have selected a spot on the green where you want the ball to land. Take a few practice swings until you find a length that you sense will hit the ball to this spot. A few minutes' practice will tell you how far the ball travels through the air for various lengths of backswing.

Because the chip is played when there are no obstacles between you and the hole, the height and flight of the shot is dictated by the loft of the club you select. Thus you need little or no wrist action when chipping. You play pitch shots, however, in a wide variety of situations that call for different degrees of height and distance. For example, if the ball has to be pitched over a bunker with the pin set close to the edge of the green on the near side, a soft lob shot would be required. This involves positioning the ball well forward at address, opening the clubface, and keeping your hands level with the ball at address and impact. On the other hand, if you were playing a longish pitch shot into the wind, you would need to move the ball back at address, hooding the clubface slightly by keeping your hands well in front of the ball at address and impact.

A steep, downward hit is necessary to pitch effectively, and that requires more wrist action than in the chip shot stroke. The set-up is very much as for the chip – feet close together, stance slightly open, weight on the left side, and hands ahead of the clubface. But that is as far as the similarity goes. In the pitch-shot backswing, the wrists should cock easily and remain cocked throughout the downswing – your left hand must 'lead' the clubface through impact.

Beware of trying to scoop the ball into the air by leaning back on the right foot and hitting upwards with the clubhead. Set your weight on your left foot, keep it there, and hit down into the ball – the loft of the club will get it airborne rapidly.

Many golfers seem to have the erroneous idea that pitching well involves 'cutting the ball up' – swinging into the ball from outside the target line and holding or 'blocking' the face of the club open at impact. This is certainly a useful shot in certain circumstances, as when the ball must fly high and stop virtually in its own pitch mark, but it is not an easy shot to play and requires considerable confidence.

Too many people try to play every pitch shot this way, and thus turn a relatively simple shot into a difficult one. Watch any of the world's great wedge players and you will see that they most frequently 'draw' the ball into the pin – moving it slightly from right to left – and yet still make it spin back off the second bounce. They achieve their stopping power much more through backspin – created by a sharp, accurate, downward hit – than by a high trajectory.

The technique for the chip shot is very close to that for the pitch, with one vital difference; whereas the pitch shot requires a free cocking of the wrists in the backswing, the chip shot requires more of an arm swing – although the wrists should never be rigid. Assuming you have a good lie, the chip shot is a firm, controlled *sweep* with the arms and club working as a unit, with just a little 'give' in the wrists and hips to prevent the action from being jerky or wooden.

One point I would stress again to sum up concerns the path of the swing. Although the club swings straight back from the ball initially, it soon must move *inside* the target line if we are going to be able to swing it straight through the ball at impact. Since the followthrough is often curtailed on short shots, 'inside to straight-through' is a good mental picture for the club's path on chip and pitch shots. If you are a confessed bad short-game player, I am sure that 'seeing' the stroke this way will help you.

The Lob Wedge

There has recently been a vogue for carrying three wedges: pitching wedge, sand wedge and lob wedge of 60-degrees or more loft. I think this is an excellent idea and have done so for 50 years or so. The reason I discarded the 2-iron in favour of a third wedge was that I could play the ball back in my stance and hit a 2-iron shot with a 3-iron, so it was easy enough to create a vacancy in my bag.

I have always been a believer in a close graduation of distances in the shorter clubs because it is more difficult to play half and three-quarter shots close to the green. So it is always better to a play a full shot into the green; hence the value of having a larger range of clubs to accommodate smaller graduations in distance.

Be competitive when you practise

Nobody has ever mastered the game of golf, or come remotely close to perfection. It is possible to imagine that a great champion will arise who splits every fairway with booming drives and hits his irons with uncanny precision. Some golfers have briefly come so close to that level of control that they could, in the words of Tom Watson, smell total mastery in those areas of the game.

But the greatest of players always have, and always will have, plenty of scope for improvement in the critical departments of pitching, chipping, and putting. These are the skills that offer the best opportunities for saving strokes. Oddly enough, they are commonly the neglected part of a golfer's game when it comes to practice. Well, it is not so odd perhaps, since practising these little touch shots does not give the golfer that tingle of sensuous satisfaction at hitting a full shot flush off the sweet spot. Chipping and putting practice soon gets boring. And if you are bored you do not concentrate properly, so the practice does not do you any good.

The answer is to make it competitive. Then it's fun. Then it does you good. When I do team coaching the players are subjected to a tough regime of serious practice followed by a round on the course. But I think they get the most value, and certainly the most enjoyment, from our evening contests.

Each day I mark out tee areas around the practice green for specific holes. The players put their entry money into a hat and play winner-takes-all. The rules are simple. One penalty stroke if your chip does not pitch on to the putting surface. And one club and a putter only. I nominate which club must be used. Each day I choose a different club.

With every team, of every nationality, this is the most popular element of the coaching week. I am convinced that it does them the most good. And as a valuable bonus, the fierce but friendly competition fosters a wonderful team spirit among players who may have arrived as strangers.

A simple tip for chipping

In order to make the ball travel upwards, you have to swing the club downwards. A good swing thought is to try to finish with the clubhead low to the ground when you play a regular chip shot. This encourages the correct, slightly descending angle of attack and keeps your hands ahead of the clubhead – a combination that helps eliminate the danger of you scooping at the ball.

Here's a useful pitching drill. Place a second ball roughly eight inches behind the object ball. To avoid contact with that second ball, the clubhead must travel into impact on a descending angle of attack. If you combine that with a slightly open clubface and keep the body moving, thus avoiding independent hand and wrist action, you'll learn to hit wonderful soft-landing pitch shots.

Texas Wedge

Don't be frightened to take a putter from off the green, if circumstances make a lofted shot more difficult. Obviously, if the grass is thick on the fairway or apron, or the ground is broken or muddy, the percentages are with a *slightly* lofted shot. If the ground is clean and smooth, by all means use a putter. Tournament pros know that a bad putt will almost always finish better than a bad chip, under these conditions. So should you.

Soft hands give your chipping more feel

Nick Faldo has often been accused of being mechanical, but I don't agree. Certainly not when you look at the way he plays little chip shots and pitches, where I think there's great fluidity and softness to his technique.

That's because although Nick is a very strong, muscular individual, he has wonderful touch. For a start he has a great looking grip, which he applies to the club with just the right amount of pressure. It's a soft, but secure hold. And although I know Nick then likes to feel that the trunk of his body controls the motion of his swing, his hands and arms stay so soft that the club flows back and forth ever so smoothly and very correctly. It looks, feels, and is, extremely controlled.

When you practice your chipping, try to adopt a posture whereby the hands and arms hang free from tension and keep your grip nice and soft. Then, as you swing the club back with your arms and shoulders, feel a little bit of 'give' in your wrists as the club changes direction from back-swing to downswing. That 'lag' effect is exactly what you want, and is created by the shoulders unwinding through the ball. It establishes the correct angles in your wrists and helps to make sure your hands lead the club into impact – striking it sweetly but still with a sense of authority.

No sloppiness, no mishits, just perfect ball-turf contact. And the great thing is, you can apply that technique to any club from a 6-iron to a sand wedge to produce a whole range of shots around the green.

Fire your imagination

Gary Player has always been a great, great bunker player. At the peak of his career, he was in a class by himself. One of the reasons he became so good from sand was the way he practised. He used to throw a handful of balls into a bunker and then play each one as it lay. So often we lesser mortals place balls in the sand on a perfect lie and show off our skills, but when faced with something a little unusual we're suddenly not so good. When Gary practised it didn't matter if the ball was buried, lying perfectly, or on some sort of slope, he'd just deal with it. That gave him the physical skills and, just as importantly, the wonderful imagination that often separates the great from the good.

This was the philosophy he applied to practising every department of his game. He'd spend as much time being creative as he would being conventional. I remember when we were both playing in a tournament at Crans sur Sierre in Switzerland, each night before it got dark we used to go to the course with just a putter and a wedge and take it in turns nominating shots – the idea being to get up-and-down in a pitch and a putt. We would start out with fairly orthodox shots, then become increasingly creative as our skill and imagination cried out for greater challenges.

My advice to you is practise like Gary Player used to. If you're working on your bunker play, don't set yourself up with a perfect lie every time. Chuck in a dozen or so balls and play each one as it lies. Bear in mind that the standard greenside splash bunker shot requires a combination of an open clubface and an out-to-in swing path, taking a portion of sand from under the ball without hitting the actual ball.

Learn how to adapt that technique to suit different situations. In a fried-egg lie you need to take more sand and generate more force, but still play with an open clubface. If the ball is completely plugged, you need a steep angle of attack and a square clubface. On any kind of slope you need to alter your weight distribution at address to vary the angle of attack – favouring the back foot on an upslope, and the front foot on a downslope. By giving yourself these shots to play, you soon learn how to deal with them.

And feel free to carry this varied approach right through your entire game. Ideally, get together with a friend and call different shots, just as Gary and I did. If you're on your own, call the shots yourself. This kind of practice fuels your imagination and develops your technique – together that helps take your game on to a new level.

Chip with arms, but add wrists to pitch

In chipping you need minimum height and maximum roll, so you should swing the club predominantly with your arms. Sweep the ball forward with little wrist action. In pitching, you need plenty of height but no roll, so you should use more wrist action to make the ball rise. But in both shots, the clubface must never catch up with the hands until after impact.

In both pitching and chipping, the length of the shot is determined largely by the length of your backswing. Too short a backswing will lead you to stab quickly at the ball, but swing the club too far and you'll tend to slow down before impact.

In your mental picture of the shot you will have selected

a spot on the green where you want the ball to land. Take a few practice swings until you find the length that you sense will hit the ball to this spot. A few minutes' practice will tell you how far the ball travels through the air for various length backswings.

Stand open . . . but not across

Your body does not need to coil and uncoil for a chip or short pitch shot – you swing the club primarily with your hands and arms. But you do need room to swing your arms past your body, and opening your stance – pulling your left foot back a little – helps you clear your left side.

The danger is that you may also set your shoulders 'open' to the target line by instinctively matching your alignment to your stance. When this happens, in trying to swing the club straight back along your target line you will actually have to pull it 'inside' relative to your shoulder alignment. More often than not the result will be a 'rebound' that throws the club outside the target line on the throughswing. This is the chief cause of the most common short game fault – pulling the ball left.

Find the perfect swing length

A successful pitching method relies on you generating a length of swing and degree of body turn that enables you to accelerate into the ball with authority, whatever distance pitch shot you are hitting.

To that end, try this exercise. Go out on to the range with just your wedge and a dozen or so balls. Give yourself a comfortable distance, say 70 yards, and hit the first couple of shots with a distinctly longer swing than you would usually make. Follow that up with a couple of shots using what feels like a much shorter swing than normal. Repeat the process a couple of times.

What you are looking for is a length of swing that isn't so short that you struggle to generate sufficient speed, but neither is it so long that you are afraid to hit the ball. The ideal length swing should enable you to swing down with natural acceleration, producing what feels like solid ball-turf contact and the ideal distance for the shot you are hitting.

The good pitcher finds a length of swing that promotes natural acceleration through impact.

How to play the basic bunker shot

It is sometimes said that splashing the ball from sand is the easiest shot in the game. I don't go all the way with that idea, but I would agree that given a basic understanding of the problems and methods of getting the ball out of sand, the average player can at least overcome the fear that seems to paralyse him every time his ball lands in a bunker. And that alone will give him a 50 percent chance of getting out of the sand with only one blow struck.

The basic splash shot is a relatively easy shot to play, *once you've established confidence*. If there is a secret to playing the splash shot, it lies in knowing how far behind the ball to apply the clubhead and then having the confidence to do it. In this shot the ball itself is never contacted by the clubface. The sand is struck behind the ball and the sand wedge, due to its heavy protruding flange, splashes or skids through the sand beneath the ball, which flies up out of the bunker literally on a cushion of sand.

How far behind the ball should you hit the sand? The exact distance depends on the flight required and the condition of the sand, and you can only learn to judge these two factors through practice and experience. But the distance will vary between two and four inches, the less sand generally being taken, the farther the ball must travel.

As in every golf shot, the correct set-up is vital. Position the ball opposite the left heel and make sure that both your feet and shoulders are set open – your left side pulled back from the target line. Open the face of the club, fractionally for a normal trajectory, wide for a higher shot. Then swing the club smoothly along your shoulder line, i.e., out to in.

I repeat, *smoothly along your shoulder line.* Make a full, free swing with the hands and arms. There need be no deliberate turn of the shoulders, but your knees should be flexed and your upper body relaxed.

In order to hit under and through the ball, you must be sure to get your hips moving and turning to the left as the clubhead swings down and through. Only by moving the hips can the face of the club be kept open, so that it slides through the sand under the ball. If your hips are static, the downswing becomes a movement of the hands and arms only. Then, as the clubhead approaches the ball, the arms start to move around the body and the clubface closes and digs into the sand. Don't swing *at* the ball – think of skimming the clubface through the sand *under* the ball and floating it out. The shot is a gentle splash, not a thunderous blast.

In bunkers, control distance by your set-up

You can govern the distance you 'splash' the ball from sand by a very simple graduation of your set-up geometry. For a very short shot, aim your shoulders well left of the pin and your clubface well to the right of the pin. For a little more distance, narrow the angle between your shoulders and the clubface. For a longer shot yet, narrow the angle even more. It is absolutely vital, of course, that you swing the club up and down along your shoulder line – not along your target line.

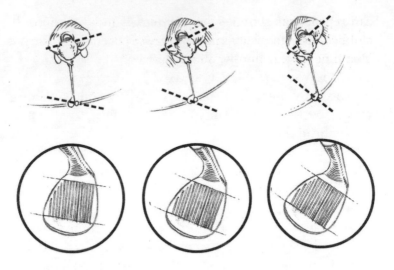

Vary your set-up geometry to control ball flight, progressively more open the closer you are to the flag.

Knife down and under a buried ball

Any time your ball is buried in the sand, the only sure way to get it out is to swing the clubhead well down and under the ball. The easiest way to do that is close the clubface so that its sharp leading edge will 'knife' through the sand when you swing sharply down behind the ball.

'Crisis management'

If you suffer from a total lack of confidence with bunker shots, I recommend you practise in sand without a ball. Open the clubface at address and make long, smoothly accelerating swings. Get used to the sensation of the clubhead sliding through the sand, not digging into it. If you can repeat that action when there's a ball lying there, the clubhead design of the sand-wedge will do the rest for you. You'll never fear bunker shots again.

CHAPTER 4

The Art of Putting

'See' the line and 'strike' the ball

Putting is not golf: it is a game within golf. How good you are at hitting the ball through the air bears little relation to how well you can roll it along the ground. Putting is largely a matter of instinct, touch, and nerve. Thus if you are naturally a good putter, nothing – and I mean nothing – should persuade you to change your method or your approach to this part of the game. If you can get the ball in the hole when it matters, how you do so is of no consequence.

Unfortunately, the better a golfer becomes at the through-the-air game, the more important his putting becomes. If you hit a green 500 yards away in four strokes and get down in one putt, you are pleased. If you hit it in two strokes then take three more to hole out, you are incensed. Most golfers never totally evade putting problems. The following is for this unfortunate majority.

It seems to me that golfers who putt poorly, especially if they miss the short ones, do so above all else because they lack *authority* of stroke. Nervousness, pressure, lack of confidence, lack of concentration, the general tizz that this game can wrap us in, leads to indecisiveness about line and distance; and, worse still, about striking the ball. We tend to wave at it, coax it, steer it, drag it, jab it, twitch it – anything but hit it.

Consequently, the poor putter needs, first, a mental resolution, a determination to strike the ball with the putter-head; and second, a method that encourages him to do so. The first is a question of total mental committal to a particular line. Sometimes we can 'see' the line better than at other times. But, whatever you do, you must commit yourself totally to strike the ball in a certain direction.

The shortest route to an authoritative strike, I believe, is to hit the ball against the left wrist, never past it. On short putts the left wrist never quits nor bends at any stage of the forward stroke. Some golfers may interpret this as a stiff-wristed action. It isn't. There is a wrist break going back, but none going forward, so that the clubface never gets ahead of the hands until well after impact.

As we get farther away from the hole, there is a 'softening' in this kind of action, of course. The strike becomes more of stroke, the arms swing farther and more freely on the backswing, and the hands at some stage pass the left wrist on the followthrough. But the principles remain the same.

Swing putter back inside line to stroke ball on line

You've probably heard or read that you should 'take the putter straight back from the ball' and 'keep the blade close to the ground'. Short of using a very contrived stroke

– and risking a body sway – these two pieces of advice are incompatible.

If you swing the putter straight back along an extension of your target line, it will naturally tend to raise well above the ground. You can only keep the blade close to the ground by swinging it back 'inside' your target line, on all but very short putts.

If you do literally force the putter straight back, it will frequently rise so high that you risk chopping down on the ball, rather than stroking it solidly forward; and you will also tend to pull the ball left by returning the putter-head to it across the target line from out to in. The fact is that, to swing 'straight through' the ball, you must allow the putter-head to move naturally 'inside' the target line on the backswing.

NB. The use of the long, or broomhandle, putter has changed things somewhat in terms of the path of the stroke. Because the shaft is more vertical at address, the putter-head tracks a straighter path back and forth. It is, in essence, more pendulum-like. Of course, these putters might not be in use forever!

Never up, never win

How often have you had the experience of everything resting on the last putt of the match and watching your partner belt the ball so hard that the ball races past, or even clear over the top of the hole? He then turns with a soppy expression of contrition on his face and tries to excuse his imbecility by saying: 'well, I had to give it a chance'.

That is exactly what he did not do. The ball had no

chance of dropping at that speed. The hoary old expression 'never up, never in' is frequently trotted out on these occasions, adding banality to injury.

Some, like Gary Player, have the courage to rap short putts so firmly that they can be hit straight into the hole, ignoring any breaks. Most of the great putters, including Bobby Jones and Bobby Locke, played their putts with just enough speed to die the ball into the hole. This policy makes the hole much wider on short putts.

On long putts, most good players concentrate on distance above all and try to get the exact speed to carry the ball up to the hole and no farther. If the ball should drop then that is a bonus, but it is not the original intention. The control of speed, or weight, is the vital factor in judging the amount of break the ball will take. On the longer putts distance is more important than direction.

A quick way to develop authority of strike

Take too long a backswing and you may unconsciously decelerate the putter-head prior to impact. This is one of the commonest causes of feeble putting. I increase my own authority of striking very quickly, if I practise putting on the carpet at home with a book placed so that it severely limits my backswing.

Putting's correct impact factors

There have been lots of better players than Ben Crenshaw in the last century, but there really hasn't been a better putter. He has a very distinctive stroke. He stands very tall, his arms relatively straight, and from there he pivots his body. His arms and the putter move directly in harmony with that pivot. There are no abrupt movements, the putter changes direction very smoothly and accelerates gradually as it strikes the ball. It's all very much one-piece, with no independent hand and wrist action.

Ben himself has said: 'I try to build my putts around pace' and an inside-to-square method, which he adopts, is great for achieving this because it encourages the putter to swing freely. The essence of Ben's success, though, is that he manages to get the putter swinging through the ball along the correct line, with the putter-face square to that line, travelling at the right speed for the distance the ball needs to roll to the hole. These are the impact factors of a great putter at work.

The key message is that you don't necessarily have to putt like Ben Crenshaw, but you do need to be conscious of those all-important impact factors and go about fulfilling them in a way that feels most natural to you personally. I don't believe in suddenly changing your method because you see someone on television 'putting the lights out'. Be yourself when it comes to putting.

Hit 'em quick

I would hesitate to recommend Colin Montgomerie's method of putting to anyone who doesn't already find it a very natural way of putting. However, getting away from the technical side for a moment, one of the things I really do like about his putting stroke is the no-nonsense way he gets on with it. Once he's over the ball and is committed to the line, it's 'one look, bang'. No hanging about. I think that's a good way to putt, mainly because the longer you stand over a putt the more chance you have to tense up or talk yourself out of holing it.

Next time you have a spare few minutes, go on to the practice putting green and give Colin's 'one look and hit' method a try. Make up your mind on the line before you are over the ball – and I mean really commit yourself 100 percent to that line. Then once you're over the ball, see the line and hit the ball along it. Strike a good putt and leave the rest in the lap of the Gods. You can do no more than that.

One final thing. Under no circumstances should you ever deviate from that routine. Many times I see people take twice as long over a crucial putt, which usually means they don't hole it. Look back to the penultimate hole of the 1997 US Open, when the gallery distracted Colin as he was about to putt. Now that wasn't Colin's fault, but it knocked him out of his usual routine, and in my view that's why he missed the putt. And it virtually cost him the championship. So try to stick to your routine at all costs. You'll putt better for it, I promise you.

If you cannot see a definite break on a putt, you must commit 100 percent to straight. Decisiveness is the best policy.

Groove perfect putting rhythm, like Arnie

Arnold Palmer was the boldest putter I've ever seen. He charged his putts at the hole, without a second thought for the one coming back. He was just so confident. There was a real sense of acceleration through the ball. It's one of the reasons Arnold holed so many putts in his career – the ball was struck so firmly that it fought to hold its line all the way to the hole.

Arnold's putting stroke wasn't only positive, it was also perfectly timed. There was a wonderful rhythm to it. People talk about rhythm in the full swing, but it's just as important with the putter. The putter should flow back and forth, smoothly but with good rhythm and acceleration through the ball.

Good rhythm in your putting stroke stems from the correct length backswing. If the backswing is too short, you have to really hit at the ball to create sufficient speed for that putt. If your backswing is too long, you have to decelerate to avoid hitting the ball too hard. Work at developing a length of backswing that enables you to swing the putter into the back of the ball with natural acceleration. Your stroke should feel positive and purposeful, but at the same time very rhythmical.

As you make practice putting strokes, try to feel the length of swing that will send the ball the required distance. Then repeat that stroke and let the ball get in the way of the swinging putter-head. If your stroke is smooth and rhythmical, I promise you will be surprised how quickly your judgement of pace improves.

NB. Arnold had a very wristy stroke, which worked wonderfully on the relatively slow greens that were typical in his heyday. Today, wristy strokes are less popular and that is purely down to circumstance. Greens are so much faster these days that a less wristy, more arms-and-shoulders-dominated stroke is more effective and consistent.

Find a pace that suits you . . . and stick to it

Think about what sort of putter you are. Do you feel more comfortable lagging your putts or do you prefer to charge them at the hole? If you have a preference, commit yourself to sticking with that at all times, whatever the circumstances. Don't be influenced to putt another way. That can be disastrous.

In-to-straight

If the putter-shaft were fitted absolutely at right angles to the clubhead we could take the club straight back and straight through with a perfect pendulum stroke. But the rules say that the shaft has to be set at an angle and we must accommodate that angle by taking the clubhead back slightly on an inside arc. The return swing is from in-to-straight through the ball.

NB. I would refer you once again to the comments on the broomhandle putter, earlier in this section.

You can't hit what you can't see

Tiger Woods holes so many crucial putts it's incredible. Mechanically, I can't fault his stroke, so let's focus on something positive that might help you hole more putts. One of the things I know he used to work on with his then coach Butch Harmon is the position of his head, specifically making sure that his eye-line is parallel to the target line at address. Also the way he looks at the hole, swivelling his head rather than lifting it, to see the line. Perhaps you've not considered that, but I tell you it can make a mighty difference to the number of putts that start on the correct line.

Also, next time you practise your putting adopt your normal address position and make sure your eyes are over the ball by dropping a second ball from the bridge of your nose. Address the ball on the spot where it lands.

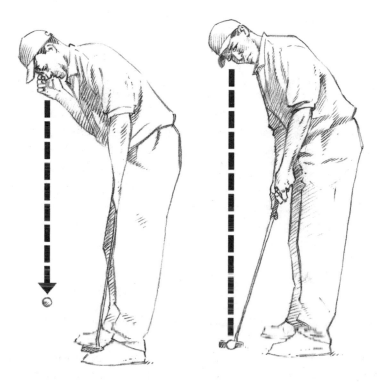

Make sure your eyes are over the ball, and that you swivel, rather than lift, your head to look at the hole.

Set hands parallel to putter-face

There are no 'musts' about grip and set-up for putting – if whatever you do now works consistently, stick with it. But if you are an indifferent putter, try setting your hands on the putter so that they are parallel to its face, and positioning your eyes over or slightly behind the ball. These are two factors common to most of the better putters among tournament professionals.

'Hit and hark' on your putts

The head is important. It must be kept really still if the ball is to be struck firmly and accurately. Set your head in one spot and hold it there as long as you can. Try to 'hit and hark'. Strike the ball and wait to hear it drop in the hole before you look up.

The final countdown

One final thought. Always try to spend at least five minutes putting before an important round – and practise the middle and long-distance putts. This is the best way to induce rhythm and feel. If you practise short putts without being under pressure to hole them, you are apt to miss a few simply because they aren't important, which does nothing for your confidence.

Take the break out of short putts . . . if you have the nerve!

At his peak, Tom Watson was one of the greatest holer-outers I've ever seen. It wasn't just the fact that he seemed to hole every putt he looked at. It was the way he holed them. Bang! Straight in the back of the hole. You'd swear he was trying to dent the back of the cup.

Tom's entire short game was brisk and positive, so there's no doubt in my mind that banging in the short putts was very much his style. It was also a reflection on the amazing confidence of the man. As he said himself once: 'I was amazing. I aimed the putter and I knew the ball was going right along that line.'

The advantage of this style of putting is that it eliminates break on all but the most severe slopes. You hardly ever have to start the ball outside the hole. I think to a degree if you eliminate break on a putt, you eliminate doubt. If you give Tom's method a try, make sure it's not on the first green of the monthly medal, but on the practice green so that you get accustomed to striking the ball more firmly from such short range.

What putter to use?

The choice of putter is highly individual. A mallet is often thought to be best for slow, wet greens; a blade for smooth, fast greens. Probably the best answer is to use the putter that gives you the best feel, or the one in which you have the most confidence. But don't stick with it if your putting goes off. I'm a great believer in changing putters if I'm putting badly. However, if you follow this advice and have more than one putter, make them as different as possible from each other. A blade and a mallet are good alternatives.

CHAPTER 5

How to Cure Golf's Most Common Faults

How you will be taught

Throughout the year I teach many groups of golfers who have gathered from all over the world to improve their golf game. On the first morning of such a school, I sometimes perform a little demonstration on the lesson tee that always seems to capture the students' attention.

First I ask a volunteer to step forth from the group. I ask for someone who has played the game for some time but who I have never before seen swing a club. Then I step to the forward part of the tee and off to one side. Facing down the range with my back to that pupil, I ask him or her to hit some shots down the range in full view of the entire class. I watch only the flight of the ball, not the player's swing, for one or two shots. Then, while I continue to look away from the pupil, I will ask one of my assistants to see that the student makes one or two simple adjustments.

Inevitably, the pupil's shots improve immediately. Someone who has sliced his drives all his life suddenly hits a shot that draws from right to left. Others who have frequently lobbed tee shots high into the air a relatively short distance now drive the ball forward on a much more penetrative trajectory an additional 20 or 30 yards.

The reason for this demonstration and my purpose in describing it here, is simply to show that the golf ball itself is your best instructor. It is the teacher *extraordinaire* for two reasons (apart from its obvious availability).

First, the ball is extremely truthful and candid, often brutally so. It never lies or misleads (as golfers do, inadvertently, to themselves). It tells you straightaway on every shot exactly what your clubhead was doing at impact.

This is extremely vital information. Above all else it forms the basis for any meaningful, lasting improvement in your game.

The messages that we take from the golf ball are visual. We see its direction of takeoff. We see its direction and degree of sideways curve. We see its upward and downward trajectory and the distance it travels.

One of my main objectives is to help you translate these visual images. I hope to explain how you can learn from what your golf ball does. I will also suggest how to apply this knowledge, not only to improve your shots generally, but also to avoid those extended periods where they go from bad to worse.

It is an unfortunate fact of golf that one bad shot frequently causes us to make incorrect adjustments. These lead to other, even more disastrous bad shots. This compounding of the original error is, indeed, a curse that all too often plagues the relatively unenlightened weekend player.

The best golfers also make bad shots. However, because

the ball's flight alerts them to the true problem, they can usually correct the error early on, before it becomes compounded.

The second reason why the golf ball teaches so well is that it is free of preconceived notions about golfing technique. It does not care if you hold the club 'weak' or 'strong'. It doesn't know or care if you align to the left or to the right. It isn't concerned if you play it forward in your stance or back. It doesn't even care if you keep your left arm straight or retain your wrist-cock late.

No, all that matters to the ball is what your clubhead does to it. Your shots, for good or bad, are determined by your impact conditions. Was your clubhead moving to the left or right, or straight down your target line when it encountered the ball? Was the clubface facing to the left or right, or straight down that path? Was the clubhead moving down, up or parallel to the ground at impact? Was it travelling at a relatively fast or slow speed?

This is not to say that we do not determine our impact conditions by the way we hold the club, set up to the ball, and actually swing. We certainly do. The point I'm stressing is that the ball can help enormously to show you what you should change in your own technique in order to improve your shots. It is a far more personal guide than some rigid gospel that is meant to fit all players into the same mould. Thus I feel I shall be in partnership with the ball to help you improve, just as I am when teaching face-to-face.

Each of the following lessons contained in this chapter follows the same format – diagnosis, explanation, and correction. Since I cannot be on hand to observe your shots, you will need to diagnose yourself to some extent. To help you do this, I will start each lesson by describing a certain pattern of shots or a certain shot making situation. If this diagnosis fits your particular situation, then the accompanying explanation and correction will apply to you.

The explanation portion of each lesson will, again, deal primarily with the influences of the club on ball. I try to make your task of understanding and applying the correction portion of each lesson as easy as possible. I often include a shortcut practice tip that will further simplify your efforts. Finally, where applicable, I will also describe the pattern of shots that will result if you do, in fact, overcorrect.

Feel free to refer back to the text and illustrations on pages 26–32 in this book showing the 'flight of the ball' which will help your appreciation of the advice in this section.

The slice

Diagnosis: Long shots generally start left and then slice to the right. The slice is most prominent with the longer clubs. Your full shots with the short irons tend to start left and continue in that direction with little or no curve to the right, as does the occasional shot with a longer less-lofted club.

Explanation: Because we stand to the side of the ball, we must swing the club forward on an in-to-in path. It must move from the inside – your inside – of the target line during the downswing and then arc back to the inside during the followthrough. Thus it must be moving towards the right of target on the downswing and the left of target on the followthrough.

The fact that your shots start to the left indicates that your clubhead is not reaching the ball until it has already begun its return to the inside in the followthrough portion of its arc. The contact is too late in your swing. This late contact will occur if you are playing the ball too far forward, too far to the left, in relation to yourself.

The fact that your long shots curve to the right is further indication of a forward ball position. When shots curve to the right we naturally tend to start aiming the club to the left. Aiming left automatically sets the handle end of the club farther to the right, behind the ball, when the club is soled. Since we tend to position ourselves according to where the handle is, we thus place ourselves too far to the right of the ball as well. Thus the ball is too far left, or forward, and late contact is all but assured.

Moreover, with the ball forward we are forced to address it with our bodies, especially our shoulders, aligned too far to the left of target. This alignment makes us grip the club with our hands also turned too far to the left. This is a grip position that leaves the clubface open to the right of its path at impact and thus reinforces the tendency to slice.

Correction: Play the ball farther back – less to the left – in your stance. This change of position might well need to be several inches. As a result of this change, your shoulders will automatically want to align more to the right. Encourage this. Similarly, your hands will want to be returned farther to your right (clockwise) on the club. Again, make a conscious effort to let this happen.

From this new address position you should be able to see the path along which your clubhead should return to the ball – that being a path that is from *your* side of the target line. See that path before you swing on every shot. Thereafter, merely swing the club freely, up and down along that path, with your arms.

If your shots should begin to start out to the right of target, you will know that you have overcorrected and that your club is now reaching the ball too early in your swing. Simply set up to future shots with the ball a bit more to your left, until you find the position that sends it off toward your target.

. . . and the hook

Diagnosis: Long shots tend to start out to the right and then hook sharply to the left. Full shots with more lofted clubs also fly from right-to-left but with less curve. Shots with any club may occasionally start to the right and continue on that line without curving. Your drives may fail to get airborne, thus forcing you to use a more-lofted club on tee shots.

Explanation: Remember, because we stand to the side of the ball, during the forward swing the clubhead must arc from the inside during the downswing and then back to the inside during the followthrough. Thus it will be moving toward the right of target on the downswing and back to the left of target during the followthrough. It will be moving on target for only a brief span between downswing and followthrough.

The fact that your shots usually start to the right of target tells me that your contact with the ball occurs too early in your forward swing. Your clubhead is still moving to the right during the downswing portion of its arc, before it has had time to reach its on-target phase.

This early contact may well occur because you are playing the ball too far back (too far to the right) in your stance. The fact that your shots generally curve left further indicates this possibility. Setting up with the ball too far to the right is typical of golfers whose shots have tended to finish to the left of fairways and greens.

These golfers invariably aim the club farther and farther to the right to offset the expected hook to the left. Aiming to the right, however, automatically sets the handle end of the club farther to the left, ahead of the ball, when the clubhead is soled. Since we tend to position ourselves according to where the handle is, these players automatically place themselves too far to the left of the ball. Thus the ball is too far right, or rearward. Early contact, with the clubhead still moving to the right, will occur unless the player somehow alters its path during the swing.

Moreover, with the ball positioned rearward the player is forced to turn his body, especially his shoulders, to the right as he addresses the ball. This alignment to the right also forces him to grip the club with his hands turned too far to the right. This is a grip position that tends to close the clubface to the left of its path by impact and thus reinforces the tendency to hook.

Correction: Play the ball farther forward – more to the left – in your stance. This change of ball position will allow you to align your shoulders more to the left, as you should do. It will also allow you to turn your hands a bit more to the left when setting them on the club as, again, you should do.

Your new address position should give you a somewhat different view of your target line as you address the ball. This line should appear to extend somewhat to the left of where it had been. Keep this new target line in mind and try to swing the clubhead along it through the impact area.

If your shots should begin to start out to the left of target, you will know that you have positioned the ball too far to the left, so that your club is reaching it too late in your swing, by which time it has already started arcing back to the inside. Merely address future shots with the ball a bit less to the left until you find the positioning that starts your shots off toward your target.

Slices and skies

Diagnosis: Your long shots have a general tendency to slice from left-to-right, and occasionally you chop under the ball and lob it upward – especially when it is teed – or top it along the ground to the left. Also, there is a general lack of distance, especially on your long shots.

Explanation: If your shots follow this pattern, I would wonder if perhaps at some time in your golfing career you had been warned against 'casting' the club from the top of your backswing – 'hitting from the top'. Or perhaps you were encouraged to 'lead with your legs' or hips in your downswing. Or maybe you have tried to emulate the famed 'late hit' position that we see in the photos of good players as they near impact with their wrists still cocked.

Such advice is fine for some. It *is* possible, and harmful, to uncock the wrists too soon. The legs and hips *do* have an important role to play. The late hit position *is* ideal, if you also have the ability to square the clubface at impact.

However, almost any piece of golfing advice can cause trouble if carried to an extreme. In recent years the emphasis on using the legs and lower body, along with

116

dire warnings against hitting from the top, has had just this effect on all too many players. Such advice has led to general overuse of the legs and body and too little appreciation of the hands and arms. Thus I find that most of my first-time pupils tend to swing *themselves* instead of the club.

The pattern of your shots tells me that you are one of those players. Your shots start left because your clubhead is moving across your target line in that direction, on an out-to-in path, at impact. Your long shots thereafter curve to the right because your clubhead is facing to the right of its path. You chop under tee shots and top other shots to the left because your club's angle of approach to the ball is too steeply downward, an inevitable result of swinging out to in. Your lack of length of long shots indicates a relatively slow clubhead speed, apart from its obvious mishitting of the ball.

These problems of impact all result from the way you start your downswing. Instead of swinging the club freely with your arms and hands, you are clinging on to it with your hands while your legs and body unwind to the left. Unwinding while clinging, instead of swinging, forces your club to move outward before it can start downward; hence the out-to-in path and the resulting steepness in the angle of approach.

With the hands locked and without the arms swinging, neither can do their part in squaring the clubface at impact. Instead, it must lag too far behind the legs and hips and thus arrive at impact with its face still open to the right.

Swinging yourself instead of the club robs you of length because your clubhead cannot move at its own maximum speed. Instead, that potential becomes limited by its too-close association with your slower-moving body action.

Correction: Hit practice shots with your feet together, actually touching. Make sure you initiate your downswing with your hands and arms. Even feel that you are casting the club, swinging it freely without overusing your body. In your case this is not an incorrect feeling to cultivate. It will give you the free swinging of the arms and free release of the hands that all good players have developed naturally, almost without effort, early in their careers. You too must develop this free swinging if you are to ever transmit fully the power of your body to the clubhead and the ball.

Once you can feel yourself swinging the club freely with your arms and hands – you will no longer be falling off balance through overusing your body – then gradually widen the stance. If your old shot pattern returns, go back to this feet-together drill until you recapture this feeling.

The push

Diagnosis: Drives start out to the right of target and curve farther right thereafter. Shots with the shorter irons also push to the right, but with little or no curve. Contact on iron shots tends to be either fat, with turf taken behind the ball, or thin, with no turf taken at all.

Explanation: I would say that the shots just described are fairly prevalent among nearly good golfers. I see two or three players in this pattern every time I walk up and down the line at my golf centres. Occasionally, you see the same pattern even among very good players.

The problem usually stems from the misconception that the path of the golf swing swing should be from in to out, with the clubhead moving toward the right of target at impact. With this idea in mind, the player makes such an effort to swing into the ball from the inside that he leaves his left hip in the way. His left leg and side stiffen and block, making it impossible for him to 'close the door' so that the clubhead can return on line at impact, with the clubface squared to that path and that line as well.

The ideal clubhead path through the hitting area is not in-to-out, but rather in-to-in. The clubhead should move *from* the inside, then briefly *along* the target line, and then back *to* the inside.

When the path is in to out instead, shots start out to the right because the clubhead is moving in that direction at impact. The blocking and stiffening of the left side that so often coincide with swinging in to out impede the arms from freely squaring the clubface, hence the open face at impact and the resulting curve to the right. Because the in-to-out path also causes a very shallow angle of approach, with the clubhead reaching the bottom of its arc relatively early, contact is often made with the ground behind the ball (fat shots) or with the ball after the club has already started moving upward (thin shots). The tighter the lie of the ball in the grass, the more damning the in-to-out path becomes.

It is only natural that many golfers feel the swing should be in to out. At some stage of the downswing we all reach a 'black out' point, a time when everything is happening so fast that we lose recognition of what is actually taking place. Because this occurs during the downswing, when the club is ideally, still moving from the inside, we tend to assume that it continues moving toward the outside after impact.

It is also natural that golfers who think 'in-to-out' will fall into an additional trap when their long shots start bending to the right. These golfers may assume that slicing results from an *out-to-in* clubhead path, as in fact, it often does. Naturally these players then make an even greater effort to swing even more from in to out. This makes 'closing the door' even more difficult and further aggravates the problem.

Finally, golfers who think of the swing as being in to out also tend to play the ball too far back to the right in the stance. This rearward positioning of the ball allows them to align their shoulders to the right so that they can more readily swing from in to out. Unfortunately, with the ball too far back in the stance, the clubhead reaches it too early, when the clubface is still open and the path is in to out. The player has not had time to turn and clear his left hip to the left, which would bring the path from inside to straight and the face from open to square.

Correction: Bear in mind that the golf swing is in to in, not in to out. Set up with the ball a bit farther forward in your stance. Then make a conscious effort to turn and clear your left hip to the left early in your downswing. In other words, 'close the door', so that at impact your swing path is from inside to on line, rather than in to out. The clubface, which is allied to the swing path, will thus square up at impact.

If your shots should begin starting to the left and, perhaps, curving to the right thereafter, you will know that you have begun to play the ball too far forward in your stance and/or failed to swing the club freely down and through with your arms and hands, as you cleared your left hip. You should then consciously swing the club *down* as you clear the left hip.

Topped fairway shots

Diagnosis: You occasionally top your fairway shots along the ground and somewhat to the right of your target line. Sometimes you catch turf behind the ball. You make your best shots when the ball is teed or sitting up well on fairway grass. Distance is not your worry, but you probably hit some of your chip shots and many of your sand shots 'thin'. In fact, the short game is where you suffer the most.
Explanation: Unlike the golfer who tops shots to the left because of an out-to-in clubhead path and a steeply downward angle of approach, the shot pattern just described indicates an in-to-out path and an angle of approach which is too shallow. The clubhead reaches the bottom of its downward-upward arc before impact and is actually moving upward when it contacts the ball. Thus it has scraped the ground behind the ball and/or caught the top of the ball while moving upward.

Because the clubhead is moving upward by impact, these golfers make their best contact when the ball sits on a tee or high on fairway grass. They hit behind or top the ball that rests low in grass or sand.
Correction: Play the ball slightly farther forward in your stance – a bit more to the left. This will allow you to address the ball with your hips and shoulders aligned more to the left as, in your case, they should be.

This alignment will make you more conscious of your ball-target line. During the backswing, swing the club up along this line with your arms, making no effort to pivot. Clear your left hip as you swing the club down to the ball with your arms.

These adjustments will make your clubhead path on line, rather than in-to-out, at impact. Thus its angle of approach will be level or slightly downward rather than upward. The bottom of your arc will occur at the ball, rather than behind it.

Also, bear in mind that an in-to-out path is usually the result of a previous tendency to hook. Should that tendency reoccur, adjust your grip by turning both hands to the left at address.

The shank

Diagnosis: You frequently shank shots sharply to the right with the shorter iron clubs. The shots you do not shank usually finish left of target.

Explanation: The shanked shot is struck on the hosel (neck) of the club, rather than on the clubface. The club has moved outward during the downswing, farther away from the golfer than it had been originally positioned at address.

This outward movement on the downswing occurs because the overall swing is too flat. During the backswing the club has swung too far around and behind the player and insufficiently upward. Thus, during the downswing, it has moved too much around the player and forward – beyond the ball – instead of sufficiently downward.

The flat swing originates from the golfer's address position. He has seen or heard that good golfers hit their shorter irons from an open stance – as, indeed, they often do. The left foot is set farther back than the right from the target line.

Mistakes occur, however, when the shoulders are similarly aligned far around to the left, rather than parallel with the target line. This alignment also forces the ball to be too far forward in the stance, to the left of where it should be.

Since so much of this game is reaction, the address position I have described leads to far too much effort being made to get the club back to the inside so as to avoid hitting to the left where the player has aligned. This effort to get inside is bound to result in a backswing that is too flat. The club finishes the backswing while moving around and behind the player. Then it rebounds around and outward, beyond the ball, during the downswing. This creates the shank.

If the shot is not a shank, it is invariably a pull or a pull-hook to the left of the target. The shot flies left because the ball is positioned too far left in the stance. By the time the clubhead finally reaches impact, it is already moving back to the inside, to the left, on the followthrough portion of its in-to-in arc. The clubface may also be closed to the left at impact, because the flat swing often makes it turn to the left too abruptly through the hitting area.

Correction: First bear in mind that the correct backswing is not only to the inside, but upward as well.

Play the ball farther back to the right in your stance so that you can align your shoulders on target, rather than far to the left. This alignment to the inside will also eliminate the need for any conscious pivot to the right during your backswing in order to swing the club to the inside.

It will also allow you to visualize a path extending from

the ball to the inside of your target line. Merely swing the club freely upward and downward with your arms and hands along the path that you have visualized.

Hitting off the toe

Diagnosis: Many shots are struck on the toe, or outer end, of the clubface.

Explanation: There are two distinctly different causes of hitting the ball off the toe of the club. The direction that your toed shots curve will tell you which explanation and correction apply in your particular case.

If your toed shots curve to the left, you will know that your clubface is closed – facing to the left of its path – at impact. When the face is turned to the left, the toe leads the heel into the ball so that contact is made on the former.

If your toed shots curve to the right, you know that your swing is too upright. In that case your situation is the converse of the flat-swinging player who tends to shank shots off the opposite end of the clubface. As I explained in that lesson, the flat-swinging golfer over-pivots during the backswing. Thus his club swings too far around behind him going back and, in reaction, too far outward in front of him going forward. The club moves out beyond the ball so the contact is made on its hosel.

Conversely, the upright swinger whose shots are hit on the toe does not swing the club *far enough* behind himself going back. Thus it does not move sufficiently outward in front of him going forward. Only the outer, toe portion of the clubface, gets back to the target line and the ball.

Correction: If your toed shots curve to the left, you will need to adjust your grip to eliminate the early closing of the clubface. Set your hands on the club with each turned a bit farther to the left.

If your toed shots curve to the right, you will need to modify your posture at address so that you can swing on a less upright plane. Increase your knee flex slightly and decrease the amount that you bend your back and neck forward. This posture will allow you to turn your right shoulder away to the inside – rather than rock it upward – during your backswing. As you turn to the right, swing the club up and inside so that it finishes above the point of your right shoulder rather than over your head.

Fat or thin contact on pitch shots

Diagnosis: Inconsistent contact – fat or thin – is made on short approach shots.

Explanation: Of the four impact factors, the most import-ant on these shots from around the green is the clubhead's angle of approach to the ball.

On these relatively simple strokes, most weekend golfers can swing the club on more or less the right path and align the clubface more or less square to that path. (And even an open clubface is not likely to spin the ball sideways an appreciable amount on these short shots.)

Now, most mishit shots occur because the clubhead reaches the bottom of its arc before it gets back to the ball. It may touch down and snag in the grass behind the ball – the fat shot; or it may skim the middle or top of the ball while moving upward – the thin shot. In either case it is the club's level or upward, rather than down-ward, angle of approach that causes the poor contact.

While the obvious solution is simply to swing the

clubhead somewhat downward to the ball, this is difficult for many golfers to do consistently until they first eliminate any need, conscious or subconscious, to 'help' the ball into the air by swinging the clubhead upward to it.

Correction: Always visualise the shot you want to play *before* you choose a club. Consider the lie of the ball in the grass, and the distance and terrain between it and the flagstick. Decide where you want the ball to land. 'See' the trajectory that would fly the ball to that spot and, thereafter, cause it to bounce and roll to the hole.

After thus visualising the shot, decide which club would most likely create it. Do not choose that club, however. Instead select a club with *more* loft than you think you need, one that will fly the ball *higher* than you want the shot to fly.

In short, eliminate beforehand any need to help the ball into the air.

Finally, set up to the shot so that you can contact the ball with a downward moving clubhead. Play the ball far enough *back* in your stance (to the right) with your hands far enough *forward* of it (to the left) so that you must catch the ball during your downswing, before the clubhead reaches the bottom of its arc.

The ball will fly into the air, even with the clubhead moving downward, because you have chosen a club with more loft than you really need.

Poor putting

Diagnosis: Generally poor putting. Seldom do your long putts approximate the right distance. No confidence on the shorter putts.

Explanation: If your putting fits the above diagnosis, it almost follows that your technique will be at fault. To show you what I mean, I would ask that you stand and face a wall. Position yourself about arms' length from it.

Extend your arms towards the wall and start clapping your hands as you do when applauding. As you clap, gradually widen the sweep of your arms. I'm sure that this will all feel natural. Even a small child can clap his hands soundly together.

You will also notice that, as you swing your hands farther and farther apart, they also move farther and farther away from the wall. This, too, is natural. And this movement away from the straight wall should similarly happen whenever we swing from alongside a target line, as we do on golf shots.

Because we stand relatively close to the ball when putting, the distance that our arms, hands, and putter-head should swing to the inside of our target line is very slight, even on very long putts. It is, however, natural – and therefore vital – that the putter does swing somewhat to the inside on all except the very short putts.

To prove this to yourself, merely clap alongside the wall once again. This time, however, make sure that your hands do not move away from the wall as they swing apart. You will immediately feel inhibited. You will feel muscular tension. You will find it more difficult to make your hands clap soundly together.

Swinging the putter on line throughout your putting stroke similarly takes away from your natural gifts. One of these natural gifts is to square the putter-face to your putting line by the time contact occurs, just as you squared your palms to each other when clapping. Another natural gift is to swing the putter-head into the ball on a relatively level angle of approach, so that the ball will roll smoothly forward without first hopping or skidding. Another natural instinct is to release the putter freely into the ball at the right speed to make the putt go the correct distance.

All of these natural and correct instincts tend to lessen whenever we contrive a putting stroke that is unnatural. As clapping alongside the wall has shown, the putting stroke that is on line throughout is, indeed, unnatural.

Correction: First hold the putter with your palms facing each other and aligned with the putter-face, just as they would be if you had clapped them together. Also stand 'square', aligned parallel to the line on which you intend the putt to start.

Next practice making strokes in which the putter-head gradually moves inside the line during the backstroke, retraces that path back to the ball and, thereafter, continues forward along the line. (On long putts the putter-head will, eventually, return inside on the followthrough.)

I suggest that you practise these strokes alongside the base of a wall. There it will be apparent when your putter-head fails to swing to and from the inside. Outdoors you can do this same drill alongside the shaft of another club that you have laid on the ground. You will eventually find how much you need to be inside on the backstroke in order to swing on line through the ball position.

As you make these strokes, learn to feel the difference between a natural and correct stroke from inside to along the line, and the unnatural on-line or across-the-line strokes. Accept the fact that the natural stroke, though correct, may feel unnatural for a time if your previous stroke was unnatural.

Finally, I would add that the face of the club should remain square to the clubhead path – not the target line – throughout the stroke. This, too, will happen naturally, as in clapping, with a little practice.

Inconsistent bunker shots

Diagnosis: Inconsistent bunker shots. Some stay in the sand, many fly over the green.

Explanation: Straightaway I should warn you against trying to pick the ball clean from the sand around the green, as many weekend golfers attempt to do. This approach presents a problem that even expert golfers avoid. The problem is simply that these are short shots. Thus they require a minimal amount of clubhead speed if the contact is to be clean. If any sand is taken, as usually happens, the club is not moving fast enough for the ball to carry forth from the bunker.

The wise golfer avoids this whole situation by making a fairly long and authoritative swing, even on extremely short bunker shots. His shots do not fly too far, however, because the clubhead never actually contacts the ball. Instead, it swings into the sand well behind the ball. It displaces a cushion of sand which, in turn, displaces the ball. The ball flies free of the bunker while riding on this cushion. It does not fly too far because this same cushion, interfering as it does between the clubhead and the ball, also deadens the force of the blow.

While swinging the clubhead into the sand behind and under the ball's position is the preferred technique, it does require a steeply downward angle of approach. If the approach is too shallow, it may not displace enough sand to cushion the blow; the ball will fly and roll too far. Or the shallow approach can cause the clubhead to skim into the sand too far behind the ball and then rebound upward into the top of it. The topped shot rolls only a few feet forward.

Remember golf's impact factors and the relationship between clubhead path and angle of approach. The more the swing path back to the ball is from the inside of the target line, the shallower the angle of approach tends to be. The more the path is from out to in, the steeper the angle of approach becomes.

Thus, since the steep angle of approach is best for penetrating sand behind the ball, the out-to-in clubhead path is best on most bunker shots. A normal swing path, such as might be ideal on drives and most fairway shots, creates an angle of approach that is simply too shallow for the normal sand shot.

If your sand shots vary from being too short or too long, especially if they tend toward being too long, it is quite possible that your clubhead path is too much from the inside, thus making your angle of approach too shallow.

Correction: Address the ball in the sand as you would for playing a fairway wedge shot, but align your shoulders farther to the left of target. Also, aim the clubface to the right of target.

Aligning to the left will help you swing in that direction, as you should do. This out-to-in clubhead path will help provide the steeper angle of approach.

Aiming with the clubface open offsets swinging to the left; the shot flies on target. Also, the open clubface allows the lower back flange of your sand iron to readily glide forward through the sand, much like a rudder, without cutting too far in despite the initially steep penetration.

There is an angle formed between the lines that indicate shoulder alignment to the left and clubface aim to the right. As a general rule you will find that the larger you make this angle at address – i.e., the further you align left and aim right – the shorter distance the ball will travel with a given force of swing (refer to illustration on page 94). Thus by increasing this angle you can actually swing quite aggressively, even on very short greenside shots.

Summing up: Clubface open, shoulders open at address. Swing the club up and down along the original shoulder line with the hands and arms. Clear the left hip to the left while swinging through to allow room for the arms to swing on the desired out-to-in path.

Bunker shots come up short

Diagnosis: Bunker shots from around the green often finish short of the target. Clubhead cuts too far into the sand.

Explanation: If cutting too far into the sand is your problem, I would first ask if you do, in fact, use a sand-wedge on these shots. If not, the club that you do us is probably a large part of the fault.

The bottom edge of the sand-wedge angles upward slightly from back to front. The bottom edge of the pitching-wedge angles downward, as do the soles of all other fairway irons. It is the upward angle of the sand-wedge that keeps this club from penetrating too far downward into the sand when it is used correctly. Because it can displace a relatively shallow cut of sand, it loses relatively little clubhead speed in the process. Enough remains to readily displace both sand and ball.

The downward angling of the fairway iron, however, makes it cut too deep into all sand except that which is exceptionally hard-packed or wet. The deep cut leaves too much sand between club and ball, and too little clubhead speed to displace either readily.

Thus the sand-wedge can be a valuable tool, especially if you must play often from bunkers that are filled with soft sand.

If you already use a sand-wedge but still cut too far under the ball, it will be a closed clubface that is largely responsible. Even the raised leading edge of the sand-wedge becomes turned downward when the clubface is closed to the left. In effect, the sand-wedge then becomes a pitching-wedge.

Correction: You may be able to avoid the closed clubface and its penetrative effect if you merely aim the clubface to the right of target while aligning your shoulders – and then swinging – well to the left.

If you should continue to cut too far under the ball, however, you will also need to stress clearing your left hip to the left while swinging through. This will bring your clubhead through the sand trailing your hands and with the clubface still open. This open clubface will keep the sole angled upward. Thus, after initially penetrating the sand, it will gradually level out and glide forward instead of continuing downward.

Poor contact on putts and half shots

Diagnosis: Occasional spells of poor contact on less-than-full approach shots and putts. These shots usually finish well short of the hole.

Explanation: Length of backswing, while not a particularly significant measure of good golf on the full shots, is an important factor on these shorter shots.

On full shots we tend to make about as much backswing as we sense we can comfortably control. This seldom requires much conscious attention. We simply swing our normal length.

On less than full shots, however, we need backswings of more specific lengths. The length should be such that, with normal acceleration thereafter, the ball will go the correct distance.

A backswing that is too long will, of course, send the ball too far if the contact is solid. More often, however, a too-long backswing breeds a decelerating forward swing that misconnects with the ball.

A backswing that is too short – the more common situation – invariably causes a quick overuse of the body during the forward swing. We tend to apply ourselves to the shot to make up for the lack of backswing that we sense. Solid contact is all too rare.

Correction: First you must discover if your backswing on these shots tends to be too long or too short. If it is too long you will, upon reflection, be extremely aware of having made a backswing. If your backswing is too short, you will have absolutely no recollection of your swing from the time you started the club away from the ball. I promise that this is true.

Another way to detect if your backswing tends to be too long or too short is to reflect upon the shape of your full shots. If your long shots usually curve to the left, it is quite probable that you misconnect on short shots because your backswing is too long. If your long shots usually curve to the right, beware of too little backswing on your short shots.

Once you pinpoint whether or not your backswing is too long or too short – don't be afraid to experiment – merely hit some practice shots, including putts, with backswings of corrective lengths. Your contact should improve straightaway.

Also, on these shots I suggest that you form the habit of making several, smoothly accelerating practice swings beforehand. Try to find and sense the length of swing that will make the ball go the distance in question with the club you have in your hand. You will not find, and then duplicate, the perfect length every time. You will, however, strike more solid shots closer to the hole than you had before.

CHAPTER 6

Trouble Shooting

In reading this chapter, I'd say wherever necessary please refer back to the passage earlier in the book where we discussed the relevance of golf's impact factors, namely: clubface path, aim, and angle of approach. It will help you understand more clearly the shot-making nature of this section on Trouble Shooting.

Assessing the risks

Every golfer lands in trouble. How well he gets out depends on his mental equilibrium, his common sense, and often, in the long run, his sheer physical strength.

The first rule of playing from trouble is simply to get out. This is where mental equilibrium is so big a factor. Many golfers become so angry or dismayed when a bad miss lands them in trouble that all reason departs. They call upon temper or belief in miracles to make amends. Neither are reliable factors in golf.

The first thing to do if you are in trouble is keep calm. The second is to decide what is definitely *possible* in the way of recovery, what is just *probable*, and what is *impossible*. If the situation is impossible, take an unplayable lie penalty and drop away or go back and play another ball. If it is just probable, and the state of the match or the game suggests a gamble, have a go. Most of the time, stick to what is definitely possible – even if it means, as it often does, the shortest route back to the fairway.

The deeper the trouble – grass, bushes, gorse, heather, bramble, bracken, etc – the more difficult it is to get out. In all those instances, whatever the ball lies in will wrap around the club's neck before the ball is contacted, slowing the club down, stopping it completely, or twisting the face off-line to the left.

Sheer physical strength is probably the only reliable method of shifting a ball from a really bad spot. If you lack it, play safe.

Executing various recovery shots

Most of the time, trouble means rough grass of varying depth and texture bordering the fairways. The problem here is how cleanly the clubface can be applied to the back of the ball, and how the ball will behave when grass comes between it and the clubface at impact.

Backspin is what controls a golf ball – makes it fly in a certain trajectory and stop in a certain manner – and backspin is best applied by the clubface hitting the ball a clean, slightly descending blow. Anything coming between the ball and the clubface at impact reduces backspin, thereby reducing your control over the shot.

The normal effect of grass coming between clubface and ball, because of the reduced backspin, is to make the ball fly lower and run farther when it lands.

A ball lying reasonably well in dry, light grass or semi-rough may be played normally, taking into account only the foregoing, i.e., that less club might be needed than when the same length or type of shot is played from the fairway.

If the ball is nestling down in long or lush grass, leaving no clear path for the clubhead to meet the back of it, the only way to remove it effectively is by a steep, descending blow with a lofted club. This shot should be played with the clubface opened a few degrees at address. Swing the club up with an early wrist-cock to produce a steep arc. In the downswing see that your hands lead the clubhead, and that your grip remains firm. The ball needs almost to be 'punched' out – struck a firm, descending blow. Don't worry about followthrough. Look at the back of the ball and try to get the clubface down on to it as cleanly as possible.

Although it doesn't always appear so, one of the most difficult trouble shots is that presented when a ball tees itself up in light rough – anything from half an inch, to two inches, above the ground. The great danger here lies in swinging the clubface underneath the ball, ballooning it weakly high into the air. Here, the only real safeguard is to watch the ball carefully and use a deep-faced club (the driver is ideal if distance is required).

Another poser is the ball under an obstacle such as the branches of a tree. Take a long iron, deloft it even more by playing the ball opposite your right toe, hood the club-face, and punch down into the ball, making sure that your hands lead at impact. Allow for a great deal of run.

An experienced and thoughtful golfer is always ready to make up shots to extricate himself from trouble. So long as you do not scoop or scrape at the ball, almost any sort of blow is permissible, and all kinds can be contrived to escape trouble.

A ball lying very close to a wall or a tree can be bounced off the obstacle to get it clear – but be careful it does not strike you or the club on the rebound. A ball in a bush can often be bunted out backwards between the legs by chopping down on it vertically. Reversed so that the toe points down, a right-handed club can be used to knock out a ball from a spot where only a left-handed swing will do.

You can get a lot of distance out of grass if height is not necessary by using an inelegant shot with a medium iron. Set up with the ball well back towards your right foot and weight predominantly on the left side. Hood the club-face slightly and, again, pick up the club quickly in the backswing to keep it out of the grass, then literally *smash* it down into the back of the ball with your hands and arms. This action will not produce a good looking golf shot, but it will get the ball moving on a low trajectory that *will* send it running a long way. Allow for the ball to hook.

One of the most difficult shots in golf is a short pitch from thick, lush grass – especially when there is little margin for error as often happens when a bunker intervenes between you and the pin, and the ball must fly the necessary distance but still land softly. The grooming of many American courses makes this a common problem for the US tournament professionals, and some of them have developed a rather special type of stroke to overcome it.

The essential club for this shot is a broad-soled sand-wedge; the essential attribute in the player is confidence, which comes from practice; and the critical part of the technique is to hit a little way behind the ball with an open clubface, as in a standard 'splash' shot from sand.

If you have rough close up to your greens, it would be worth experimenting with this stroke. Play the ball well forward, open the clubface slightly at address, make a slow and easy swing with plenty of arm action, the club going back a little outside the target line. Then swing the clubhead down a little way behind the ball – being sure to keep it going right through grass and ball.

What follows is a selection of other trouble shots you might encounter on the golf course.

Situation: You face a shot from a 'tight' lie. The ball rests either atop bare ground or well down in the grass.
Suggestions: In either of these tight-lie situations, your clubhead must first contact the low-lying ball, not the barren ground or too much of any grass that might be behind it.

To catch the ball first the most important impact condition to create is a fairly steep angle of approach. The clubhead that reaches the ball while still moving downward will have already passed over the bare ground or much of the grass, whichever the problem may be.

There are two excellent ways to steepen your club's angle of approach. However, each tends to create an entirely different type of ball flight. One makes shots fly a relatively short distance on a rather high trajectory. The ball settles quickly upon landing. The other method produces low-flying, running shots that travel further overall.

I suggest that in any tight-lie situation you first decide which of these two types of shot you would prefer. Then apply the downswing-steepening technique that is more likely to create that shot.

The method of steepening your angle of approach that results in the high, short shot involves swinging the club through impact on an out-to-in path. First align your shoulders farther to the left than you normally would. Then swing the club parallel to that leftward alignment through impact.

To make this shot fly on target, rather than too the left in the direction you are swinging, open the face a bit to the right at address. Set your hands a little forward, to the left of the clubhead, as well. Maintain the open clubface through impact by making sure that your hands lead the clubhead into the hitting area. Because of the open face, you should allow for the shot to curve to the right except when using a highly lofted club. The amount of curve to plan for will increase with the length of the shot.

These shots usually fly higher than normal and settle quickly upon landing, because the open clubface increases loft. The added loft will make the shot fly a shorter distance, however, as will the glancing blow that comes from swinging to the left with the clubface opened to the right. Thus a 6-iron, for instance, might easily produce an '8-iron' shot.

The second way to steepen your angle in tight-lie situations is, in fact, identical to the method I suggest for sand shots from fairway bunkers. In each case you should play the ball farther back to the right in your stance than normal. In each case you would set your hands well forward, to the left of the clubhead, in more or less their normal position relative to your left thigh.

This combination of ball back and hands forward, if

maintained through impact, assures that contact will occur before the clubhead has completed the downswing portion of its arc. To further assure a descending angle of approach, address the ball with more weight on your left side and with your right shoulder slightly higher than normal. Swing the club up and down the target on a fairly upright plane, predominantly with your arms.

This shot will usually fly lower and run farther than normal because the ball-back, hands-forward combination 'hoods' (delofts) the clubface. That same 6-iron that I said might create '8-iron' shots with the first tight-lie solution mentioned, might well produce '4-iron' shots if you apply this second approach to the problem.

Situation: Your ball is in the rough, say 4-iron distance from the green. You would like to use that club so as to reach your target. However, you have found in the past that you do not contact the ball solidly on shots from rough with longer, less-lofted clubs.

Suggestions: This is another situation where the weekend golfer often wastes strokes. He bows to the temptation to go for the green with the club that he would normally use from the fairway at that distance. As it swings into the ball, however, the clubhead snags in the intervening grass. All too often the ball finishes far short of the desired distance.

I suggest that in this sort of situation you first choose a club with more loft than you would normally use, in this case say a 7-iron instead of the 4-iron.

Play the ball further back in your stance than normal (the deeper the lie, the farther back you should play the ball and the more-lofted club you should choose). Do not, however, set your hands any farther to the right than their normal position at address.

With your hands well forward of the clubhead, you will find it easy to swing the club more abruptly upward and downward than normal. The steeper angle of approach into the ball avoids most of the grass behind it and thus makes the impact more direct.

The better contact makes the shot go farther. So too does the fact that the 7-iron's steep approach has, in effect, reduced its loft, perhaps even to that of the 4-iron you would have preferred to use in the first place.

Usually the shot will fly lower than you would normally expect from the club in hand. It will generally roll much farther, however, perhaps as far as the green. Therefore you should take into account beforehand the problems posed by intervening hazards.

Situation: Some object – perhaps a tree or bush – blocks your line to the target. It seems impossible to play over or under the object. The choice is either a straight shot safely away from the problem or a curved shot around it.
Suggestions: I find that this situation causes many golfers to attempt shots that cannot possibly succeed. The shot that they intend should curve flies straight or the intended straight shot curves.

The golfer blames his poor swing on bad luck. He resolves to get it right next time. But he will fail again and again, until he finally realizes that talent alone will not succeed on some shots in golf. There are certain conditions that make certain shots all but unplayable, even for a Jack Nicklaus.

Conditions affect what your club can do or cannot do to the golf ball: *the ballistics of impact.* I want to make you aware of these conditions so that you will not attempt to avoid the object in question with a risky or impossible shot but, instead, will play the shot that conditions more or less favour.

The conditions you should consider in this sort of situation apart from any crosswind or any slicing or hooking tendency you might have, are (a) the length of the shot, (b) the lie of the ball and (c) any sloping terrain in the immediate area.

Length of shot. All things being equal, it is possible to curve long shots in either direction. Since these shots call for a minimum of clubface loft, the contact will be high enough on the back of the ball to apply sidespin.

In most instances, however, impact ballistics favour playing the longer shots from left to right, not right to left. This is true because the right-to-left shot calls for an in-to-out swing path with the clubface closed to the left of that path at impact. Since the closed face delofts the club, the straighter-faced woods and longer iron clubs may not carry enough effective loft at impact to put the ball into the air. Therefore you must be sure to choose a club with more loft than you would normally select. A 5-iron, for instance, might actually translate into a 2-iron or 3 iron at impact.

Moreover, the long right-to-left shot requires an exceptionally good lie, since the in-to-out path makes the angle of approach very shallow, especially with the longer-shafted clubs. The ball must be sitting up perfectly so that the shallow-moving clubhead can contact it solidly without catching in grass or turf behind it.

Conversely, long shots can be played from left to right with far less risk. This shape requires an out-to-in path with the clubface open. The out-to-in path creates a relatively steep angle of approach so that the contact can be fairly solid even if the lie is less than ideal. Also, since the open clubface increases loft, it becomes relatively easy to get the ball well into the air with the straighter-faced clubs. The added loft will, however, reduce the length that you can expect from the club in hand.

Short shots played around an object are all but impossible to curve from left to right. The extra loft that results from the required open clubface, when added to the already highly lofted irons, makes contact occur well to the underside of the ball. This low contact puts so much backspin on the ball that it cannot be curved to the right.

It can be curved from right to left, however, thus making this the preferable shape on short shots. With the highly lofted clubs enough loft remains, despite the required closed face, to easily get the shot into the air. Moreover, with the loft decreased by the closed face, contact occurs high enough on the ball to apply the right-to-left sidespin needed to make the ball curve.

The lie of the ball. A good lie with plenty of grass under the ball simplifies playing a right-to-left shot but makes slicing more difficult. Conversely, as I have said, the tight lie on barren ground makes slicing relatively easy but renders the right-to-left shots practically unplayable.

When the ball sits high on the grass, the human instinct is to sweep it away with a relatively flat swing. This type of swing encourages the clubface to close rapidly in the hitting area, thus facilitating the right-to-left shape. Moreover, with the ball ideally situated on the grass, solid

144

contact is possible despite the relatively shallow angle of approach that results from the in-to-out clubhead path.

When we have the opposite sort of lie, with the ball resting on barren ground, both human instinct and golf ballistics favour slicing.

First, we sense that it would be difficult to contact such a low-lying ball solidly if we made a flat, sweeping swing. Instead we tend to attack it with a somewhat steep angle of approach. This, in itself, tends to leave the clubface open at impact, just as it should be for curving shots to the right.

Second, as I have said, the open clubface needed for slicing also has the effect of increasing the club's loft. This extra loft sends the ball well into the air despite the tightness of the lie.

The tight lie, however, all but disallows the right-to-left shot, other than with the highly lofted irons. This shape calls for a closed clubface and a shallow, in-to-out swing path. With the ball resting tight to the ground, the straighter-faced club cannot make solid contact with the bottom of the ball. However, since the shorter irons force us to stand closer to the ball and, therefore, swing on a more upright plane, it is possible to make solid contact with these clubs even when the lie is tight.

The immediate terrain. As a general rule, you will find it relatively easy to slice, and difficult to hook, when hitting from downhill terrain and/or from a sidehill with the ball below your feet.

You will find it easier to hook, and more difficult to slice, if the terrain on which you stand is uphill and/or sidehill with the ball above your feet.

Situation: You face a shot from sloping terrain.
Suggestions: Almost any slope, no matter how slight, will affect the impact conditions. You will need to adjust your address position and/or your swing to take account of these special situations.

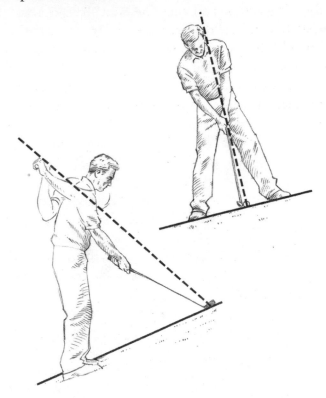

*The tendency is to hook the ball to the left on
each of these sloping lies . . .*

There are four basic types of sloping lie. There are the two sidehill situations, where your feet are more or less level with each other but higher or lower than the ball itself.

And there are the uphill and downhill lies, where your left foot is either higher or lower than your right.

Uphill lie: Hitting up slope creates the need for an upward angle of approach. This approach makes the ball fly higher and stop sooner than normal. The hillside inhibits leg action and therefore restricts the clearing of the left hip during the forward swing. Instead, the arms and hands tend to take over and close the clubface to the left prematurely. (Adjustments: Choose a club with less loft than normal. Aim it to the right of target. Set yourself perpendicular to the slope, with your right side lower and

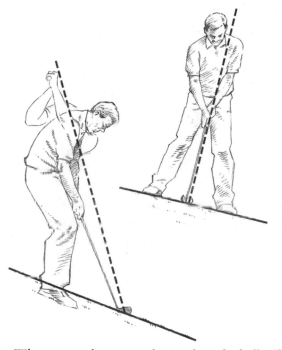

. . . Whereas on these two sloping lies, the ball will tend to slice to the right in its flight.

your left side higher than normal. Swing down the slope going back and up the slope going forward.)

Downhill lie: The downslope requires a steeply downward angle of approach. This makes the ball fly lower and run farther than normal. It also tends to leave the clubface open to the right at impact so that the ball slices in that direction. (Adjustments: Choose a more-lofted club. Aim for a left-to-right shot. Set up perpendicular to the slope – right side higher, left side lower than normal. Swing up the slope going back, down the slope going through.)

Sidehill lie (ball above feet): With the ball higher than the feet, you will need to address farther from the ball. This will create a flatter, more sweeping swing. The flatter swing tends to close the clubface to the left more abruptly than normal during the forward swing. (Adjustments: While standing on the slope, make several practice strokes until you can find and sense the flat, sweeping plane needed for solid contact. Then aim and align for a right-to-left ball flight and try to duplicate the flat swing that you sensed beforehand.)

Sidehill lie (ball below feet): A more upright swing than normal is needed for the clubhead to reach the bottom of the lower-sitting ball. The exaggerated upright swing, however, tends to make contact occur with the clubface open. (Adjustments: Stand closer to the ball and bend forward as needed for the clubhead to reach ball level. Aim and align for the shot to fly from left to right. Swing the club largely with your arms and hands on a particularly upright, straight-line arc.)

Situation: Going for distance out of sand.
Suggestions: The most important factor in going for

distance from sand is correct club selection. So often I see players with the ball lying well back in a shallow bunker take a straight-faced club, then, in mid-swing, suddenly think they are going to catch the trap's front lip. The inevitable result is that they try to flick the ball off the sand. That causes the wrists to release too early, widens the downswing, and brings the clubhead into the sand behind the ball. Disaster – always!

It is vital if you want distance from a bunker to hit ball first, sand second – just as one does with an iron from the fairway. To do that, it is imperative that you have no fear in your mind that you haven't enough loft on the club to lift the ball over the bunker's front lip. This is your limiting factor in the distance you can get from sand. You have to take the club which will, without doubt, clear the lip, even when you deloft it a little by positioning the ball farther back than normal towards your rear foot, with the hands three to four inches ahead of the clubface at address.

This set-up, with the weight predominantly on your forward foot, ensures that the ball will be hit first, sand second. From this position swing normally and forcefully, endeavouring above all to lead the clubface into the ball with your hands.

Never be overambitious on this shot. Err on the safe side.

My overall advice on bunker play is that you give a little time to practise it. Sand really isn't the terror it seems to most club golfers. If you will spend an hour hitting shots from sand, I'll guarantee your fear of it will disappear.

CHAPTER 7

Answers to Frequently Asked Questions

Timing

Question: I constantly encounter references to 'timing', but never a clear explanation of it. What is timing?

Answer: Expressed as simply as possible, the golf swing, to use one of my favourite teaching phrases, consists of 'two turns and a swish'; that is, a rotational coiling and uncoiling of the body combined with an up-and-down swinging of the hands, arms and the club, as both units are supported by the feet and legs.

When the pace and rhythm of the hand and arm action so synchronize with the body action that the club impacts the ball squarely and at optimum speed, the swing and/or the shot is said to have been perfectly 'timed'.

What that really means, of course, in non-golfing language, is that the 'turns' and the 'swish' have been perfectly coordinated.

Attempting to co-ordinate their 'turns' and 'swish' perfectly is the chief reason tournament professionals

151

practise so much, and their ability to do so is the factor most separating them from handicap players.

Here's how to identify and fix two chief 'timing' problems you'll encounter, assuming that your grip, set-up and swing mechanics are sound.

Shots sliced, topped to the left, or 'thinned'

Cause: your body is unwinding faster than your hands and arms are swinging the club down, thus preventing the radius formed by your left arm and the clubshaft at address from being fully restored at impact. This excessively 'late' hit leaves the clubface open, hence the slice, or delivers the bottom of the clubhead to the upper part of the ball in the case of the topped and 'thinned' shots.

Cure: be sure that you have not weakened your grip or are opening your shoulders at address. Then deliver the clubhead 'in time' by focusing on swinging your hands and arms down from the top of the backswing, which will automatically slow your body rotation. Apply this medicine on the 'soft' shots as well as those calling for full power.

Shots hooked, topped to the right, or hit heavy or 'fat'

Cause: you are 'restoring the radius' too soon by swinging your hands and arms down faster than your body is unwinding, causing the clubhead to have closed if it reaches the ball cleanly (draw or hook), or to be travelling upward by the time it reaches the ball (top), or to contact the ground before arriving at the ball (heavy or 'fat').

Cure: check that you have not 'strengthened' your grip or are misaiming the clubface at address. Then deliver the clubhead 'in time' by focusing on *unwinding* your hips through the ball from the top of the backswing, which will automatically slow down your hand and arm action.

Head matters

Question: 'Keep your head down,' says my partner every time I miss a shot. 'Keep your head still,' say most top players and teachers. Is this as important as everyone makes out?

Answer: 'Keep your head down and you'll keep me in business forever' has been one of my favourite sayings through all the years I've been teaching golf. The reason is that keeping the head down, to the point where the chin sits on or close to the chest, forces a tilting rather than a rotating or coiling action of the shoulders in the backswing, leading to all manner of ugly moves – and even uglier shots.

Trying to keep the head still is better than attempting to keep it down – just as long as doing so doesn't inhibit the free and fluid upward and downward swinging of the hands and arms or rotation of the body away from and then towards the target.

For most golfers, the best thought is to keep the head steady enough to permit both of the above actions with the least possible change in the axis of the body, as represented by the upper part of the spine, during its coiling and uncoiling.

Swivelling the chin away from the target just before or as you start back, in the manner of Sam Snead or Jack

Nicklaus and many other top golfers, promotes freedom and fluidity of motion while keeping the axis steady.

Straight or cupped under?

Question: What position should the left wrist be in at the top of the backswing?

Answer: I am often asked, mainly by good players, what I think to be the best position at the top of the backswing; whether to have the left wrist straight, or whether to have it cupped under the shaft.

Let me begin by making it quite clear that I think it of no importance – provided the position used fits the rest of the swing. Great players have used both positions. It is largely a question of which is the most natural to the person concerned. Some individuals can indeed vary this position at will, but others are stuck with what they do naturally.

The left-hand grip has a definite bearing on what position the hands will be in at the top of the backswing. If the left hand is put well over – i.e., showing three knuckles at address – it is more likely that the left wrist will cup under the shaft at the top of the backswing; this is so because the left thumb is more out of the way and the hand is more over the shaft, so that the wrist is more free to break across the back of the hand.

This type of grip pretty well necessitates this top-of-the-backswing position, too, in order to keep the blade open enough. Put very generally, a three-knuckle grip will tend itself to shut the blade of the club, but will be balanced by a complete underneath wrist-cock at the top of the backswing, which will tend to reopen the blade.

A grip, on the contrary, which has a left hand showing

*A strong left-hand grip (centre) requires a cupping
of the wrist at the top (right) to square the clubface.
A weak grip requires no such action (left).*

only one knuckle at address, will tend to stiffen the wrist-cock at the top, since the left wrist will cock *against* the left thumb – thus producing a straight left wrist at the top of the backswing. This type of grip does not necessitate the cupping of the left wrist, since the clubface will be open enough naturally.

Generalising, then in the orthodox type of backswing we have two distinct patterns. One with the left hand showing only one knuckle at address, usually producing a straight left wrist at the top of the backswing; and the other with the left hand much further over at address, necessitating a cupped left wrist at the top of the back-swing.

Should you be the type of player who suffers by present-ing the clubface to the ball incorrectly, don't be afraid to experiment with your grip and with the resultant wrist action. Normally, if the left-hand grip is moved to the left and the wrist action stays the same, then the clubface will be more open at the top – other things being equal – than it would if the left hand were further over the grip at address.

At times, however, a left hand placed a little further over the shaft, and thus producing a fuller cocking of the left wrist at the top of the backswing, can produce a more open-clubfaced swing. This is often the case with players who feel the only way to open the clubface is to show no knuckles at address with the left hand; from this position the left wrist usually goes very flat and locks at the top of the backswing; so that, in spite of the grip, the clubface will be too shut.

Great players have, of course, used many combinations of grip and wrist action. From no-knuckle grips and a cupping of the left wrist at the top of the backswing – which has produced a very open-clubfaced position requiring lots of wrist flick and roll in the hitting area – on the one hand, to four-knuckle grips and no cupping of the left wrist at the top of the backswing – which of course produces a very shut-faced position, requiring all push in the hitting area, and corresponding body action to make this possible.

The intelligent player decides what is needed, what is most natural for him to do, and therefore which is easiest to change. For example, if you naturally flick and roll in the hitting area, this will need an open-faced top-of-the-backswing position. On the other hand you may have been trying to flick and roll to get the blade square if it has been *too* open.

This is where a change of grip, and therefore of your top-of-the-backswing position, may be the answer.

Conversely you may be a 'pusher' in the hitting area; in this case the face will not need to be as open, but make sure you are not just pushing the ball only because the clubface is too shut at the top to allow you to do otherwise!

I have tried to show how one must balance the grip with where one arrives at the top of the backswing, and in the hitting area. If something is wrong, try to decide which of these things would be easiest to change, to get the desired result.

Some years ago the great Ben Hogan described his personal 'secret' as a cupping of the left wrist at the top of the backswing; thus, I venture to say, he opened his clubface more than it had ever been before, enabling him to get away from the tendency towards hooking the ball, which had always dogged him before. Obviously, it was by experimenting that he found that little thing out. If you're not too happy with your own game, do try and do likewise: *experiment*.

The Arm Swing

Question: What role do the arms play in the golf swing, relative to other parts of the body?

Answer: The arms must be swung freely to play good golf, but never to the point where their motion gets out of sync with the coiling motion of the body in the backswing and its uncoiling in the downswing.

During the backswing the arms swing up as the body rotates away from the target, then during the downswing the arms swing down as the body rotates towards the target.

Some good golfers feel that their bodies coil in response to the swinging of their arms, while others feel that their arm swinging is generated by the coiling of the body. Either feeling is fine, just so long as it produces complete co-ordination of the two actions – that is, does not cause one to lag behind or get ahead of the other at any point during the swing.

To witness how freely the arms of a really fine golfer swing the club to the ball, stand facing him and watch the space between his hands and right shoulder during the downswing (refer once more to the illustration on page 63). You will hardly believe how fast it widens. Now watch that friend of yours with the larger handicap and the even larger slice. Because he spins his whole upper body mass into the shot before he swings his arms downward, the space opens much more slowly.

Leg and Hip Action

Question: How much should I use my legs and hips, and what should they do?
Answer: During the backswing you should use your legs and hips to resist the rotation of your upper body, but *only to the degree* that you are still able to set the club at the top on a plane and in a direction that produces correct impact.

Get the balance right and your leg and hip action during the downswing will, more often than not, happen correctly and automatically. That's because setting the club correctly at the top promotes delivering it to the ball from inside to straight along the target line, which in turn promotes clearing the left side to make room for the hands and arms to swing through correctly.

Highly skilled golfers are able to restrict their lower-half backswing motion to, at most, a slight raising of the left heel, a pulling of the left knee inward towards the still-flexed right knee, and a tugging of the hips through about half as much rotation as the shoulders, while still positioning the club for correct impact.

Less gifted players usually cannot swing the club on the plane, and in the direction that returns it correctly to the ball, without 'giving' more in their legs and hips in response to their upward swinging arms and rotating shoulders. However, there must always be some resistance from below the waist, in order for the player to be able to swing the club rather than himself.

The simplest and usually the best 'feels' for producing sound leg action among the majority of golfers are of simultaneously rotating the shoulders and swinging the club up in the backswing, then of rotating the hips as the arms swing the club down and through the ball.

Hitting shots heavy

Question: Why do I hit the ground before the ball so often?

Answer: There are two common causes of this depressing disease. Among both good and bad players alike, it can often be nothing more complicated than bad posture at address, leading to loss of balance during the swing. The golfer stands to the ball in such a way – usually crouching or reaching for it – that his weight is pulled forward on to his toes. Inevitably the momentum of the downswing throws him even farther forward, with the result that he either 'falls into' the shot, or is forced to dip his head and shoulders to get the clubhead to meet the ball. To avoid such a destructive fault is just one more reason why we must always start the swing from the correct set-up, remembering particularly in this case that the back must be reasonably straight.

The most common cause of fluffing, or hitting heavy, among reasonably accomplished players is poor co-ordination of body and hand action in the downswing. It is the opposite of the topper's problem – a tendency to hit too early with the hands and wrists, before the hips have cleared a way for them to swing past the body and out towards the target.

As most slicers are prone to topping, so most hookers are liable to fluff occasional shots. What happens is that the fluffer lengthens his swing radius by letting the clubhead catch up with and pass his hands before they have arrived back at the ball. In other words, the arc the clubhead is describing as it approaches impact is too wide – the hit is too 'early' with the hands and arms. It is, indeed, to avoid catching the ground that ladies – most of whom must hit early to get the clubhead moving at maximum speed by impact – instinctively rise on their toes during the downswing.

For many golfers, however, the cure for this fault is definitely not to be found in ballet dancing. The fluffer's basic problem is to better coordinate his downswing left-hip movement with his arm and hand action – even to the point, for a time, of deliberately restricting his wrist action – deliberately hitting 'later' with the hands and wrists.

An out-to-in path

Question: Why do I hit across from out-to-in on so many shots?

Answer: By far the most probable reason is a chain-reaction of set-up errors ingrained since you first took up the game by constantly delivering the clubface looking to the right of its direction of travel, as follows *(you may want to refer again to the illustration on 'ball flight' at the start of the book)*:

• In an instinctive effort to prevent your long shots from finishing to the right, you aim the clubface to the left of your target at address.

• The more to the left you aim the clubface, the farther forward in your stance you position the ball.

• The further forward you position the ball, the more left of target you align your shoulders in order to be able to set the club behind the ball at address.

• Your forward ball position and open shoulders have the effect of 'weakening' your grip relative to your target line.

• Prevented by your open shoulders from starting the clubhead back from the ball correctly, you quickly manoeuvre it to the inside of your target line, either by spinning your shoulders or by pulling your arms in that direction, or both – probably while also fanning the clubface open with your hands and forearms.

• Reciprocating those backswing moves, you start down by throwing or heaving your entire upper body mass – shoulders, arms, club – over and around towards the target line.

- This continuing pattern of movement delivers the clubhead to the ball steeply across the target line from outside to inside.
- The clubface mostly arrives at the ball open to that swing path, producing a slice with the least lofted clubs and straight-left pulls when the backspin produced by lots of clubface loft nullifies the effect of the sidespin.

Sadly, most people who 'play' golf this way are convinced their problem lies in the way they swing the club. The truth is that it is caused almost entirely by faulty gripping, clubface aiming, ball positioning, body alignment, and posture. Learn to set up correctly. If you will thereafter concentrate only on swinging your arms 'down' from the top of the backswing, I think you will find golf more enjoyable than you ever believed possible.

An in-to-out path

Question: I'm a pretty good player, but tend to miss a lot of shots by swinging too much from in-to-out. Why?
Answer: As with the out-to-in swingers, most in-to-outers ingrain a chain reaction of set-up errors by habitually delivering the clubface looking to the left of its direction of travel, as follows *(once again, you may want to refer back to the illustration on 'ball flight' at the start of the book)*:

- The instinctive reaction when shots go repeatedly left is to try to prevent that by aiming the clubface more and more to the right of the target at address.
- The more to the right the clubface is aimed, the farther back in the stance the ball is positioned.

- The farther back the ball is positioned, the more right of target the shoulders must be aligned in order to be able to set the club behind the ball at address.
- The rearward ball position along with the closed shoulders have the effect of 'strengthening' the player's grip relative to his target line.
- The closed shoulders and strong grip promote swinging the arms too much to the inside, which causes the shoulders to tilt or rock instead of turning or rotating, with the clubface often tending to roll inward into a closed position.
- Reciprocating the backswing moves, the shoulders rock rather than rotate in the downswing, blocking the arms from swinging freely past the body. In combination, those actions cause the wrists to function independently, either rolling the clubface closed through impact and hooking the shot, or holding it open and pushing the shot.

As with out-to-inners, golfers who have ingrained an in-to-out clubhead path as a response to shots constantly finishing left are inclined to look for the solution in a different way of swinging the club. The truth once again is that the solution lies mostly in improving their set-up to the ball.

First, take the time and trouble to correct your grip, your clubface aim, your ball position, your body alignment, and your posture. Then concentrate during the downswing simply on turning your hips 'out of the way' to allow your arms to swing freely past your body, thus enabling you to hit the ball to the target rather than swing the club to the ball.

'Methods'

Question: You read and hear a lot about one top player using this 'method' and another using some other 'method'. Are there really different methods of swinging and, if so, which is the best?

Answer: Let me first remind you of an important statement:

'The golf swing has only one purpose: to deliver the head of the club to the ball correctly. How that is done is immaterial, so long as the method used permits correct impact to be achieved over and over again.'

Having said that – and while the precise mechanics of the best players' swings do and will forever remain somewhat individualistic – it does seem to me that, over the past decade or two, a greater consensus has been reached about more areas of golf technique than ever before.

A prime example is the now almost universally accepted importance of the set-up in determining how the club is delivered to the ball at impact. Another example is how much the positioning of the ball on the ground relative to the player influences the 'shape' – i.e., the plane and direction – of his swing.

My 50 or so years of teaching tells me that the concept of 'plane' has long been and remains the most confusing element of swing technique or 'methodology'.

Back in the mists of time, golfers of the feathery and gutty ball and wooden shaft eras found swinging the club fairly 'flatly' or 'around themselves' to be the most effective way of raising the missile into the air as well as propelling it forward. Then, as the rubber-cored ball and steel shaft promoted shorter and firmer swings, they also gave rise to the notion that swinging straighter – i.e., with the clubhead remaining closer to the target line or moving more 'uprightly' – would make the ball fly straighter.

Today, few top players or teachers would argue with the premise that the body must rotate at a shallower or 'flatter' angle than the arms swing up and down, for the club to be consistently delivered to the ball with its face square to the target while travelling momentarily directly along the target line and at the correct angle of attack.

The reason, of course, is that attempting to swing excessively 'straight' generates in most people a 'rocking and blocking' action of the shoulders – a tilting rather than a rotational motion – that produces all kinds of mishits by forcing the hands, wrists, and arms to work independently of what the rest of the body is doing.

In the end, each of us at this game has to discover what works best for himself as an individual by hard experience – by plain trial and error within a framework of tried and tested fundamentals.

In that regard, I believe we are at a stage in the evolution of the golf swing where combining rotation of the body with upward and downward swinging of the arms has become the universally accepted framework for that often frustrating but ever fascinating exercise.

Golf at its simplest!

Question: What's the simplest way to become a good golfer?

Answer: To play this game really well, you must first understand and accept that you will never hit a golf ball exactly as you wish every time you swing. No one ever has and no one ever will. Two of the greatest golfers in history, Ben Hogan and Jack Nicklaus, regarded a round in which they hit four or five shots precisely as they intended an exceptionally fine one in terms of ball striking.

Nevertheless, your chances of minimizing the amount you miss by – the key to *scoring* at golf – are definitely improved by *trying* to hit every shot perfectly. Here, then, as simply as I can express it, is the process that most easily and frequently produces perfect golf shots:

1. Select target and visualize shot flying to it.
2. Mind-picturing target and target line promotes correct clubface aiming.
3. Correct clubface aiming establishes proper ball position relative to feet.
4. Correct ball positioning promotes proper body alignment and posture.
5. Correct ball positioning and body alignment promote proper gripping.
6. Correct gripping, body alignment, and posture promote swinging club back in proper plane and direction.
7. Correct backswing promotes automatically swinging the clubhead through impact at maximum speed with clubface looking in same direction clubhead is travelling.

CHAPTER 8

Golfing Greats
(and what you can learn)

GASP for a better swing

Ernie Els is a big man with a beautiful-looking golf swing, much of which stems from his attention to detail at the address position. He misses nothing. The grip is perfectly orthodox, the posture totally correct and the ball position spot-on. Any golfer who gets this many things right at address can expect, and deserve, some very worthwhile benefits when the swing gets underway.

This attention to detail is lost on most club golfers – they assume someone as good as Ernie works on fancy swing theories all the time. Not so. He works on his fundamentals just like any other golfer should. In my experience, it is the club golfers who are least likely to work on these basics when ironically it is they who need to most. Over the years I've been forever reminding pupils to check their grip, aim, stance, and posture – GASP. And I'm going to do it again now.

The grip must make it possible to control the clubface for the individual. The aim of the clubface fixes the ball position and therefore the stance. Correct posture makes possible the correct body turn that creates the necessary in-to-in arc so vital in order to release the club at speed through the hitting area.

Ernie's waggle works wonders

One other thing, take a leaf out of Ernie's book and develop a pre-swing waggle. It's the simplest of movements. Just move the club away from the ball and back again by softly hingeing your wrists back and forth. A couple of those is enough and it just stops you gripping the club too tightly and thus prevents tension creeping into your hands and arms. So when your swing does get underway, the first move away is more likely to be a smooth one. That should do wonders for the rhythm of your swing.

'Hey Jack, keep your chin up'

For me personally, Jack Nicklaus is the greatest player the game has ever known, and yet as a ball striker he is vulnerable to elementary technical flaws, just as you and I are. I remember back in the 1969 Open at Lytham, I walked to the second tee and there was Jack playing a practice round with Gary Player and Gardner Dickinson. The first drive I saw him hit went miles right over the adjacent railway line. So he reloaded and then hit the biggest pull hook you've ever seen, practically killing someone standing on the other fairway! He did the same at the third. I walked with the three of them to the sixth, a big par-5, where Jack got out his driver and hit another drive at least 50 yards off the fairway on the right. At that moment, Jack turned to me and said: 'You're supposed to know a bit about the golf swing, what do you think about that?'

I'd heard both Gary and Gardner telling Jack for the first six holes to get his backswing more rounded as opposed to very upright. But as I said to Jack: 'You can't possibly get your backswing more rounded with the posture you've got', Jack said: 'What do you mean, posture?' I replied: 'The back of your neck is actually parallel to the ground'. His chin was so buried in his chest that he could only tilt his shoulders. There was no room to turn.

My suggestion to Jack was simple but effective. It would be the same advice I would give to any golfer who came to see me with a similar fault in their game. I said to him: 'Doesn't anyone ever talk posture to you Jack?' He looked at me and said: 'Well, funnily enough, every time Jack Grout [Nicklaus's long-term coach] sees me hit shots he pretends to give me an uppercut punch to keep my chin up.' I suggested to Jack that he had better start doing that pretty quickly, so we stood on the that tee for about 15 minutes and hit at least a dozen drives. This time Jack kept his chin up and his back much taller. That was all it took. Jack started to make a more effective upper-body coil, because there was room to turn his shoulders correctly. As soon as he started to make a better rotation, the plane of his swing returned to normal, which meant his left side now cleared in the through swing, allowing the hands and arms to swing the club through as opposed to being blocked.

The priorities of golf

Teachers are sometimes accused of being obsessed by technique, believing this to be the be-all and end-all of golf, and ignoring the equally important mental side of the game. In entering a plea of 'Not Guilty' to this accusation I would make one amendment to the wording of the charge. The mental side, in my opinion, is not equally important as technique. It is the *most* important element in golf. My priorities are: (i) Temperament, (ii) Technique, and (iii) Physical strength.

The golfer who completely confirmed me in my opinion was Gary Player. As a young man when he first visited Britain he had a terrible swing. I remember the late and much-lamented Leonard Crawley, a fine amateur and a good judge of the golf swing, remarking that Gary would never do any good in the game. I demurred because Gary had about him an inner fire and a lust for success that simply could not be denied. He worked at his game like a man possessed. And he sought advice from anyone and everyone he thought might help, always in the politest and most respectful of terms.

'Excuse me, Mr Jacobs, but would you mind if I asked you a question about the grip?' His very appearance, with those piercing eyes of a bird of prey, marked him out as a man of destiny. So I pointed out to Leonard that Gary had the character to make his horrible swing work, and repeat consistently, and win. After all, anyone can improve his technique but he is lumbered for life with the temperament with which he was born. And in this context Gary was a born champion.

We practised a lot together and, like everyone else he approached, I helped him as much as I could. His swing improved and was good enough to dismiss me from a matchplay tournament in the first round. The next winter I went to play in South Africa and my game went to pot. Gary was most solicitous and helped me back into the groove, to such effect that I beat him in the final of the South African Matchplay Championship. Talk about role reversal! But that little story illustrates the camaraderie that for me is the very soul of professional golf.

Gary went from success to success and became one of the Big Three. In the company of Arnold Palmer and Jack Nicklaus the diminutive Player was seriously outgunned. He determined to build up his physique and strength to the point where he could hold his own against the longest hitters in the game. He went into serious, not to say punishing training and thereby got into the habit of daily physical exercising, a habit which kept him competitive on the Senior Tour at an age when most athletes are running only to fat.

Sandy Lyle

Down the years Britain has produced some wonderful players and Sandy Lyle is a worthy successor to the likes of Harry Vardon and James Braid. Starting with the Boys' Championship, he has had great success and, thankfully, has remained totally unspoilt by them. Technically he is a bit suspect but there is merit in his taking the club back too much around the right side. This creates a tendency to come over the top, but this is a wonderful way of playing golf badly. He stands a little bit open and thumps the ball with an almighty hit down the left side of the fairway, cutting back to the middle.

During the 1988 World Matchplay Championship I was working on the new Edinburgh golf course at Wentworth when his caddie came with a request that I take a look at Sandy. To get out of the way we went over to the second tee of the East course and had a good, two-hour session. He was taking the club back very much around the right side and not only cutting the ball but, unusually for him, pulling his shots as well.

I teed the ball off the teeing ground, in a position several inches below his feet where the bank made it impossible for him to take the club back on his normal inside line. It had to go straight up as he turned his shoulders. I had to go straight off to Spain that evening and follow his triumphant progress to the title from afar. But when I returned I found waiting for me a typically generous letter of gratitude from this wonderful guy.

Ian Woosnam

For me Ian Woosnam swings the club exactly the way I think it should be swung. We are all astonished at the distances he hits the ball but, as he turns his shoulders and swings the club up at the same time, he is the perfect exemplar of the secret of long hitting: *clubhead speed correctly applied.*

Nobody applies it more correctly. It seems to me that his temperament is affected by the way he is putting, but he is the model for every young player to copy in terms of technique. He is a better Hogan, if you like – more fluid and more correct in that he does not have to drive it through and hit as late as Hogan did.

Ray Floyd

Golf at the highest level is a game for hard men – and they don't come any harder than Ray Floyd. He had a look that could wither opponents at 50 paces and next to Jack Nicklaus had probably the best temperament of any player over the last half a century. He was once dubbed by his fellow tour pros as 'the toughest man on Tuesdays' for his reputation as a ferocious competitor, before the serious business of tournament play had even started. The thing was, Ray always found practice rounds pretty mundane, so he would spice them up by placing some hard cash on the line. 'Playing for your own money is a great way to learn how to compete under the heat,' he once said.

This hard school of learning was Ray's education in the game. He'd grown up gambling on the golf course, the driving range, the putting green – anywhere you could hit a golf shot was a good enough place for a wager.

In the 1960s he soon developed a reputation as a serious hustler, frequently playing challenge matches for $1,000 a time. On one occasion he lost two consecutive games to a young pro by the name of Lee Trevino, which cost Ray and his backers several thousand dollars. The backers wanted to cut their losses and leave town, but Ray insisted on another showdown and doubled the stakes, putting in $2,000 from his own back pocket.

When he and Trevino butted heads again the next day, they came to the last hole dead level, but Ray holed a 20-foot eagle putt on the 18th green to shoot 63 and pip

Trevino by a shot. On evidence like that, it's little wonder Ray became one of golf's real hard men, as tough a competitor as you could ever dread to come up against. He was a very sound ball striker throughout his career, but perhaps his greatest strength – other than a champion's temperament – has been his short game.

In his prime he was a wonderful putter, with a distinctive style you could recognize from a mile away. He uses a longer-than-standard putter and stands very tall, more upright than any other golfer I can think of, with his hands high.

The best way I can sum up his stroke is to say that he swings his hands, as opposed to his hands swinging the putter. By that, I mean his hands swing on a consistent arc back and forth and the putter simply responds to that motion. That's a good way to putt. There is no need for manipulation of the putter mid-stroke and thus there is no need for independent hand action. You get the definite impression that everything is working together in Ray's stroke.

Is Ray's method for you? Well, I always say to my pupils that if you don't have a problem holing putts, don't change a thing. But if you feel you don't hole enough short and medium range putts, give it a go.

As I see it, there are distinct benefits to Ray's style of putting. For one thing, standing tall gives you a very good view of the hole and indeed the line to the hole. And if you can see the line, you can hit the line.

Secondly, an upright posture encourages the arms to hang down relatively freely from tension. You don't want the arms to feel ramrod straight, but instead slightly flexed with the elbows pointing in towards your body.

174

This naturally comfortable position encourages the hands, arms, and the body to operate as a team. There's less of a tendency for the hands and arms to 'fight' one another during the stroke.

Thirdly, as we've already touched upon, standing tall over the ball puts you in a super position to make a very free swing of the hands and arms. Everything flows. There is no abrupt or jerky movement to upset the path of the putter.

Ben Hogan

The story of Ben Hogan is so remarkable that it is hardly surprising Hollywood made a film about his life. As a boy he endured the agony of seeing his father shoot himself. As a young professional he struggled to make his way, before finally making the break through. Then, just as he was riding high, he was nearly killed in a car crash. He then rebuilt himself to become the greatest ball-striker who ever picked up a golf club. There'll never be another Ben Hogan.

Let me tell you a tale that illustrates how good Ben Hogan was. When he won the 1953 Open at Carnoustie – the only time he played in our championship – the draw for the last day wasn't like it is now, leaders out last. Instead, we played 36 holes on the final day and the order of play was determined by drawing names out of the hat. As luck would have it, during both the morning and afternoon rounds I was waiting to play on the 3rd tee when Hogan was hitting down the par-5 6th. The two tees are close together and I had a perfect view straight down his target line.

For those who don't know Carnoustie, there is out of bounds all the way down the left side of the 6th hole and a bunker about a third of the way into the fairway on that side. Then there is two-thirds of fairway to the right of that bunker and some shortish rough right of that. Everybody took the safe option, either aiming at the middle of the fairway, looking to fade it away from the bunker and the out-of-bounds fence, or aiming into the right-hand rough and playing for a little draw. Everybody except Hogan, that is.

He was the only man in the field who aimed at the tiny gap between the bunker and the out-of-bounds fence. His lightning-quick swing fired the ball off on that line like a bullet, and towards the end of its flight there was just the merest hint of fade which brought the ball round the back of the bunker and into the middle of the fairway. That was the only way you could knock it on the green in two that day, and he made birdie-fours both times, shot 70–68 and won by four shots.

This was Hogan at his sublime best. That year, aged 41, he entered only six tournaments and won five of them. Three were major championships – the Masters, Open Championship and US Open. How about that?

You may have seen pictures of Hogan, but you could not possibly get an idea of the speed of his swing. It was like lightning and couldn't have been in greater contrast to Sam Snead's slow, almost lazy tempo. The thing is, both players swung the club at a pace that felt right for them and, more importantly, at a pace that allowed them to stay in complete control. They also had wonderful balance.

Your best rhythm is one that allows you to generate power, while maintaining complete control over the many moving parts in your golf swing. As I've explained, everyone is different and therefore I believe that even the experienced golfer will benefit from a little trial and error in this department.

Next time you practise, hit batches of balls with different-paced swings. Start with your normal rhythm and experiment on both the fast and slow side of that. By working on different rhythms you'll soon get a feeling for the ideal blend of power, control and balance. That's the rhythm for you.

A great deal depends on the type of person you are. If you're hyperactive, a fast walker and talker, then the chances are your optimum swing speed will be on the Hogan side of rapid. If you're more of a laid-back type, someone who walks slowly and seldom gets flustered, then I would say your golf swing's ideal operating speed will be on the slow side, rather like a Fred Couples or a Vijay Singh. Lastly, fast swingers are invariably short in stature – slow swingers are usually much taller. I think this may be due in part to differences in the centre of gravity. These are mere indicators, though. The rules are by no means set in stone.

Hogan hits a shank!

One day I was in the match directly in front of Hogan. It was a treat to turn round and watch his second shots dropping time after time around the pin. There was one longish hole on the back nine where the second shot had to be laid up short of a hazard; this left a short pitch to the green. The next tee was quite close to the green. I had hit my drive and was walking off the tee just as Hogan was playing his 9-iron or wedge to the flag. He had about 60 or 70 yards to go. He hit the ball clean off the socket – right off the pipe of his pitching club. It flew sharply right and, as a matter of fact, very nearly hit me as I walked forward. I though to myself at the time: I bet there aren't many who have seen Hogan hit a full-blooded shank.

Bernhard Langer

As a boy from a poor family in Germany, Bernhard Langer was given four old clubs to play with. Three of them, a 2-wood, 3-iron and 7-iron, he learnt to wield with devastating effect. The fourth, a putter with a bent shaft, proved a little harder to master. Thus the career pattern was set for this remarkably resilient and talented golfer.

I really take my hat off to Bernhard. I can't think of a comparable situation where a sportsman has come back so many times from such fundamentally damaging technical difficulties. I'm talking about the yips, just about the worst thing that can happen to a professional golfer. To suffer them once in a career would be once too often. But poor Bernhard's putting stroke has been afflicted at least three times, the effects sometimes lasting several years.

Bernhard describes it himself as 'an uncontrollable movement of the muscles. It can go anywhere from a twitch, to a freeze where you can't move at all, to a sudden explosion.' It's hard to imagine what that must feel like, yet easy to understand the phenomenal strength of character he has shown to overcome those physical and mental obstacles.

On that basis I suppose you might say it's surprising that Bernhard went on to win twice at Augusta, a golf course with arguably the most treacherous greens in the world. But Bernhard's much publicized traumas on the greens disguise the fact that he has at times in his career been a wonderful putter. More to the point, as far as Augusta is concerned, he has also been consistently one of the best mid-iron players I've ever seen – amazingly accurate with both line and length, which means he can hit his approach shots in the right place on those vast, sloping greens thus leaving himself the most holeable putts.

This devastating accuracy is the product of a golf swing that I would describe as very sound, rather than pretty. I first met him at the Bob Hope Classic at the RAC Club in Surrey during the early 1980s. He asked me what I thought of his swing and I can remember my exact reply: 'Bernhard, don't let anyone stop you turning like that.' This was a time when due to a combination of the success of Jack Nicklaus and the way the swing was being taught, many players tended to rock the shoulders as opposed to turning them with just a degree of tilt established by the spine angle at address. So it made a pleasant change to see someone turning their shoulders correctly.

What I also said to Bernhard, however, was to 'get your girlfriend to stand just to the right of you and behind you.' I was only joking about the girlfriend, but the serious message I wanted to get across to Bernhard was that his arms were locked to his shoulder turn and he was thus swinging too flat and around himself. He needed an obstruction behind him to force him to swing his arms and the club more upwards and not so much around himself.

This isn't an unusual scenario. Often, golfers suffer from the arms being locked on the same plane as the body turn, resulting in a very flat backswing. It's a position that leaves you trapped at the top, with no room to swing the club down on the correct path, resulting in anything from a bad slice to a pull hook.

I don't suggest for a minute you get anyone, let alone your wife or girlfriend, to stand behind you as you swing. But if you suffer from an excessively flat swing it is a good idea when you practise to have some kind of physical presence to force you to swing the club up and on the inside in your backswing.

Many a time when I was swinging too flat I would make practice swings with a hedge behind me. If I could swing the club up and avoid contact with the hedge, I knew I was getting a better balance between arm swing and body turn. Give it a try, but make sure you keep turning. As I said to Bernhard, you don't ever want to lose that element of your golf swing.

Sam Snead

Slammin' Sam Snead was a poor boy from a farmer's family who developed a golf swing that was like a Rolls Royce engine; silky, smooth, quiet, powerful and purposeful. It didn't matter how many miles Sam put on the clock, his swing never seemed to miss a beat.

No other golfer lasted quite as well as Snead. At the age of 62 he almost won the 1974 USPGA Championship, pipped only by Lee Trevino and Jack Nicklaus, two golfers who weren't even born when Snead was winning his umpteenth tour event! Only weeks before, he'd finished runner-up in the Los Angeles Open, one of the biggest tournaments on the PGA Tour. He's still the oldest golfer ever to win a main tour event – the Greater Greensboro Open aged 52 – and for 20 years it was virtually front page news when he *didn't* break his age. For the record he shot a round of 60 at the age of 71, and aged 84 was still a good enough player to put together a score of 66. That is nothing short of miraculous.

I remember seeing him play for the first time and like everyone else being awe-struck by the rhythm and power of his golf swing. Sam hit it miles with that lazy-looking swing.

I can still picture one great moment during one of his practice rounds during the old Canada Cup (now known as the World Cup) played on Wentworth's West course. He was on the par-5 17th and had hit a good drive down the middle of the fairway. He was sizing up the blind shot that you have on that hole and he turned to his caddie and said, 'Whad'ya think?' in that southern drawl of his. The caddie explained that the line was straight at a particular tree on the horizon. 'One-iron?' Snead suggested. The caddie agreed. He then hit one of the most magnificent, towering long-iron shots I've ever seen. The ball never left the tree. Snead looked at his caddie and in a nonchalant kind of way just said, 'Is that about it?' An understatement if ever I heard one.

There were two key fundamentals at the heart of Sam's great rhythm. First, he had a wonderfully soft grip pressure. He always maintained that you should grip the club with the same pressure you'd use to hold a live bird in your hands – one of the most valuable and enduring lessons of all time. Secondly, Sam never tried to hit the ball too hard. Even with his driver he was never operating at more than about 80 per cent, which meant his swing would always feel under control and in perfect balance.

Try to follow Snead's example. A soft grip will free-up

the natural rhythm in your swing and introduce a sense of fluidity to your movement. And remember, the fact that the ball is positioned to the side means the arc of the swing will be through the ball from in-to-straight-to-in. Your address position should make you aware that you will be going back on the inside, so swing down at the ball from the inside and clear the left side so that the club returns to the inside in the followthrough, having delivered the clubface square and on line at impact.

As an amusing aside to all of this, it's worth mentioning the fact that Snead could be a little wild at times with his driver. One year when he partnered Ben Hogan in the Canada Cup I once heard Hogan say to Snead 'put that Goddamn driver away'. Given the stature of the man uttering the words, and the nature of the delivery, you'd be inclined to listen, wouldn't you?

Nick Price

The elements in the making of a champion are to start with the right temperament, acquire the right technique, and then work on physical strength. I have not talked about golf with Nick but you get to learn a lot about a person from watching him play and I suspect that he did not have the temperament for tournament golf when he started. But he acquired a quite superb technique, so effective that he won in spite of his temperament. And through the experience of winning developed a champion's temperament. Now he has got it all. I do not think he is particularly strong physically, but his impact is so good that he is pretty long. What a lovely person and, like Sandy Lyle, an absolute gentleman.

Lee Trevino

Born into poverty, the grandson of a Mexican gravedigger, Lee Trevino could scarcely have had a less privileged upbringing. But he hustled and fought his way to the top, becoming one of golf's truly colourful characters, not to mention one of the most gifted.

He started out collecting range balls six days a week. When he left that job and joined the US Marines, a career perhaps not best suited to his outgoing personality, Lee got probably the first lucky break of his life when a clerical error landed him in the Special Services division and he got to play golf every day with the officers. He became good, very good in fact, and after being discharged from the Marines was soon the professional at a club in El Paso. I got to know of him before he became famous, and by playing with his own money on the line he soon became a lethal competitor. It was this kind of education that bought Lee a hard edge and a tough temperament.

Mind you, it was 1968 before he made it on to the tour full time and by then he was nearly 30. Nicklaus and Palmer already had private jets and Lee was staying in cheap hotels and driving from one tournament to the next in a $1,500 station wagon, apparently frequently losing his way.

So impressed was veteran Gene Sarazen when he got paired with Lee at Westchester in 1968 that he came into the press tent afterwards and told the assembled media: 'I just played with a man you're going to hear a lot about. He's going to win a lot of tournaments.'

When he eventually did win, he did so in the biggest possible way at the 1968 US Open at Oak Hill. On the final day, with Palmer playing behind him and Nicklaus ahead of him, Lee put on his lucky colours – red shirt and black trousers – and fired a 69 to win by a shot and become the first man in history to compile four sub-70 rounds in a US Open. When asked by the press what he was going to do with his $30,000 prize, he said: 'I might buy the Alamo and give it back to Mexico.'

He's a genuinely funny guy. He was also one of the most gifted ball-strikers ever. I would go as far to say that in the late 60s and 70s he was one of the best golfers in the world. Jack Nicklaus once said to him: 'You're much better than you think you are!' His self-taught swing might not be the prettiest to grace the fairways of the world, and it certainly has taken a punishing toll on his back over the years, but my word it is effective. He could shape a shot any way he liked.

Talking of shaping shots, where the ball goes depends on what the clubface is doing at impact. From the point of view of the club golfer, any lofted club is easy to draw whereas to fade – which requires the necessary sidespin – a relatively straight-faced club is required.

These factors have a major influence if you want to shape shots. For instance, if you want to go round a tree that's blocking your path to the green and you've only a short shot to play, you would not be able to shape the ball from left to right because there would be too much loft on the club and thus too much backspin and too little sidespin. Thus from short range, a draw is a better option because this shot relies on the clubface being closed to the swing path and, of course, a closed clubface means less loft and more sidespin.

If on the other hand you have a long way to go, it's

difficult hitting a draw because as I've explained in order to shape the ball from right to left the clubface has to be closed to the swing path. And since there is very little loft to start with on a long club, you only have to close the clubface a little and you've effectively got 'negative loft'. The ball therefore won't fly. Thus from long range a fade should be your preferred option.

Bear these impact factors in mind whenever you contemplate shaping an iron shot.

Henry Cotton

Henry Cotton, my boyhood hero, was considered so great that Dunlop named a golf ball in commemoration of one his rounds – a stunning 65 in the 1934 Open Championship at Sandwich. That was by three shots the lowest round of the tournament and it just about summed up Henry in his heyday – a class apart.

My first sight of him was hitting shots with just his left arm at the 1938 Open, which my mother had taken me to. Even though I was only a boy I can remember to this day how impressed I was. There was such wonderful rhythm in his swing and such crispness in the strike. Seeing Henry play was one of the best things that could have happened to me as a young golfer. It inspired me and also instilled in me the importance of rhythm.

In a strange twist of fate, I found myself up against my hero in the final of the 1954 Penfold Matchplay tournament. I must be honest, he was still my hero even then – not the ideal frame of mind for a match! I'd been putting well and playing well all that week. The final was played in pouring rain and it was blowing a gale. Dai Rees asked me if I would be interested in splitting the combined winner and runner-up purse. I told Dai: 'If Henry agreed, I certainly would', since Henry was still someone I felt I was not in the same class as, even though he was then coming to the end of his career. I couldn't have been more surprised when Henry agreed. The trouble was as soon as I knew that I relaxed, which I believe may well have contributed to me being soundly beaten 5&4. That was a shame.

Sitting here, some 60 or so years later after I first saw him play, there's no doubt in my mind that in terms of ball striking Henry was in the top half-dozen of all time. He always used to talk about the importance of the hands. However, this overlooked one factor – namely, Henry's immensely strong legs. They were like tree trunks, providing a stable base for his swing and supporting a wonderful body action that was always perfectly in tune with his hands and arms.

And therein lies the real key. Henry 'collected' himself as he started his downswing in such a way that culminated in all the moving parts surging towards the ball as one, and arriving at impact together. No moving part worked independently of another in Henry's downswing and the result was a strike of awesome authority.

The coordination in Henry's downswing – call it harmony of movement, if you like – is a wonderful lesson for us all. You don't want to be all legs and no hands and arms in the downswing, which is what much of golf instruction in the 1960s, 70, and 80s advocated. Equally you don't want all hands and arms, and no leg action. There needs to be a balance – the body unwinding at the same time as the hands and arms swing the club down.

You should feel that as you start your downswing you collect together all the moving parts of your swing and that they arrive simultaneously at impact. That's what great timing is all about and it's amazing what a difference that makes to the quality of your ball striking.

Bobby Locke

In his dominant years Bobby Locke was a distinctly un-athletic figure with a unique swing and an exaggerated draw on his shots that probably gave the purists little pleasure. But four Open victories in under a decade speaks volumes for this mild-mannered South African's unique talent and he was undoubtedly one of the most underrated golfers of the 20th century.

I knew Bobby for many years. We first me before the war when a grand tour of challenge matches around the country brought him to my home club, Lindrick. He was a lanky, 20-year-old kid who was about as keen on the game as anyone I've ever met. He literally couldn't get enough golf. The morning after the match he dragged my cousin Jack out of bed to squeeze in another 18 holes before heading off to Liverpool to catch the boat back to South Africa. While chatting after their game together, Jack remarked: 'Young fella you've got tremendous talent, but you'll never do any good hooking the ball like that.'

In fact, Bobby carried on hooking it exactly like that for the rest of his life and it worked rather well! But while Jack's advice on the swing didn't make a lasting impression, his gift to Bobby of a pair of white golf shoes did. Bobby never forgot that gesture and after the war would insist that Jack join him for one of his practice rounds at the Open. I loved this, because I used to get in on the act too.

His iron play was unbelievable. Again he drew every shot, but whereas most hook shots tend to roll, Bobby's stopped quickly since he hit down on the ball with his huge shoulder roll, as opposed to wrist roll employed by most golfers who hook the ball. He was a wonderful judge of distance. I remember we were tied for second playing the last hole together in a tournament at Sunningdale in the early 1960s. After good drives I hit my approach shot bang on line and he slightly over-hooked his to the left of the pin. I thought 'I might have him here', but when we got to the green I was short and he was pin high and inside me. It was uncanny how often Bobby was exactly pin high. I holed my putt and he followed me in from 20 feet. That was typical of Bobby, too.

His swing was so repetitive, as I am sure were his swing thoughts, which explains how he could play so well with so little practice. I'm not kidding you, he would amble on to the range to hit a few 6-irons, a couple of drivers and a few wedges. Then on the way to the first tee he'd casually stroke a couple of putts. That was him ready for action. He never seemed to play badly. Oh, now and then he'd hit a shot that started right and didn't draw back as far as he intended, but I'm talking small margins. In just over two seasons on the US Tour, he played in 59 tournaments, won 13, was runner-up in 10 and third in another seven!

I played a lot of golf with him over the years and he really was the complete golfer. He was a very accurate driver, a great iron player, and spectacular putter. His putting stroke was like a miniature version of his full swing. It had all the same characteristics – backswing inside the line, with the downswing outside the line of the backswing, but still from the inside as the body turned through. Today on the professional tours, many putters rock the shoulders to keep the putter swinging straight back and through. Bobby was different. He turned his shoulders to hit from the inside to straight through. I'd have to say it's not a method I'd recommend in its entirety to anyone else. Nevertheless there are certain snippets that I believe we can all draw inspiration from.

In my experience, most players have a putting stroke which replicates their full swing tendencies and let me say once again that if you have found a method that works, don't change it.

What is important for every golfer to understand, though, is that the correct combination of clubface alignment and swing path is the key to success. Bobby Locke repeatedly used a stroke that applied the putter-face slightly closed at impact on a very slight in-to-out path. Conversely, a few fine putters cut their putts using an out-to-in path through the ball with an open face at impact. The strokes could not be more different, yet they each set the ball off on the correct line, consistently.

That is the crux of the matter. Even if you choose not to make a stroke that produces a perfectly on-line, square clubface at impact, so long as the face and path complement one another – as they did in Bobby's stroke – then the ball will travel on the line you intend it. Therefore you should concentrate on other key factors such as committing yourself to the line of the putt and the length of the backswing, which allows a rhythmical acceleration through the ball to achieve the correct distance.

Remember, speed determines the amount of break you

play on a putt. If you like to hit your putts firmly, or you putt mostly on slow greens, the ball will not be severely affected by the slope on its way to the hole. However, if you like to die your putts into the hole at a slow speed as Bobby did throughout his career, or you putt on slick greens, then you'll have to play a lot more break.

Peter Thomson

How good was Peter Thomson? How about that he was the only golfer in the 20th century to win three consecutive Open Championships and five in total. Impressive enough, but just look at his run of finishes from 1951 onwards. As you read this, please bear in mind that it started when Peter was only 20 years of age: T6, 2, T2, 1, 1, 1, 2, 1, T23, T9, T7, T6, T5, T24, 1, T8, T8 . . . we'll stop there in 1967, but even into the 1970s he was still notching up top-10 finishes. It is a simply staggering sequence.

In his prime Peter was a good enough player to win any tournament he showed up at, but he loved fast-running courses and therefore links golf was his forte. As he once said: 'I just happen to hit the ball low and straight, which is helpful at the Open'. Not just at the Open, either. On one occasion I can recall he flew from the States to play in a tournament at Sandmoor in Yorkshire. The course was bone hard and parched. Peter arrived too late to fit in a practice round, yet when the 72 holes were over nobody was within 15 shots of his winning total! He was that good.

I played a lot of golf with him over the years and I can tell you the best club in his bag was his temperament, no doubt about it. He was like Jack Nicklaus in that on the last few holes of a major championship, with a chance to win, he'd be the calmest person on the course. 'The super player,' he once said, 'has one vital quality: calmness.'

He had that all right. I don't think there has ever been a golfer who managed his game better than Peter. He had an enviably simple, no-frills approach, right from the way he preached the virtues of a sound set-up, through to the way he plotted his way around the golf course always keeping the ball in play. One of Peter's gifts was that he knew his strengths and limitations.

A classic example was how he so often refused to use a driver. You see, the manner in which he swung meant that he presented the clubface to the ball in a strong position – in other words, deflofted – so the ball flew low and ran a long way. That made it difficult for him to flight a driver correctly, so he seldom carried that club. Some might have considered that a distinct disadvantage and remodelled their swing in order to be able to hit a driver, but not Peter. He refused to change a swing that was perfect for 13 clubs, just to be able to use a driver. In Peter's mind, power always played second fiddle to position.

It's not the glamour side of the game, but developing a shrewd sense of strategy is the club golfer's most direct route to consistently lower scores and more trouble-free rounds of golf.

The purpose of the tee shot is to get yourself in play and in a position that makes your approach shot as straight-forward as possible. The realistic aim of your approach shot is not to hole it, but to avoid potential hazards guarding the green and at the same time give yourself a holeable putt. And so it goes on. One smart shot benefits the next. I think if you were to go out in your next round of golf and play every hole with position, not power, in mind, you'd avoid the disaster holes and shoot lower scores.

Above all, know your limitations and play within them. Remember, a good round of golf isn't just about the great shots you hit, it's as much about the bad shots you don't hit. Peter knew how to stay out of serious trouble. Even when he did make a mistake it rarely became a disaster, he always seemed to be able to recover or at the very least consolidate. His equilibrium was totally unshakeable.

Nick Faldo

As a young boy Nick Faldo dismantled a perfectly decent bike in order to find out exactly how it worked. Many years later he did the very same thing to his golf swing and put it back together to become the most successful British golfer of the 20th century.

He started playing golf when he was 14 years of age and within four years had won the English Amateur Championship and the British Youths, along with eight other amateur titles in a ten-month winning spree. Two years later he won the prestigious PGA Championship and later that year in his first Ryder Cup singles match beat the reigning US Masters and Open champion Tom Watson. By 1983 his stroke average had plummeted to just about bang-on 69, the lowest of any golfer in the world that year.

Despite the success, Nick knew he could do better and I suspect his painful back nine collapse in the 1983 Open, when he had a sniff of victory, merely hammered that point home more forcibly. 'I've been close in a couple of Opens and not been able to finish the job,' he said at the time. 'The problem is my technique, or lack of it.' When he joined forces with David Leadbetter, in my opinion they started working on exactly the right things straight away. I have to give great credit to David for the manner in which he taught Nick. He really did a wonderful job. Of course, it was a courageous decision of Nick's but absolutely the correct one. I strongly believe he'd have struggled to win one major, let alone six, with the swing he had in the early 1980s.

By the late 80s and early 90s you'd have had a tough time convincing me that he wasn't the best player in the world. Six major championships in less than a decade is a fantastic strike rate. He's also won more Ryder Cup points than any other player in history. I've always been impressed with his single-minded and dedicated approach to his golf. This work ethic and unflinching desire for perfection enabled him to make the absolute most of the enormous talent he showed as a youngster. Nothing, as far as Nick was concerned, would get in the way of his goals.

Nick's swing changes centred around a few key elements of his swing. He widened his stance a little so that his legs would stabilise and support a more rotary body action. He then focused on winding his body over a more passive leg and hip action, which created resistance – in effect, energy that he would then use to drive a more powerful downswing. The arms swung in response to the body motion, whereas in his swing of old, the hands and arms dominated the action and the body just went along for the ride. Basically, Nick went from being a very handsy player to a more body-controlled, passive-hands player.

That was just the ticket for Nick, but overemphasis on body action is dangerous territory for the average golfer because it assumes you have a great hand action and, to be frank, most club golfers suffer from a lack of hand action rather than too much.

That's why I often prefer to use the arc of the swing to get the body moving. This medicine will be good for your swing if you tend to hit the ball very high, often hitting a push with a left-to-right shape, mixed with the occasional snap hook. Once you get the correct in-to-in picture of the swing path, your body will clear out of the way virtually automatically and thus you won't need to drive the legs to avoid coming over the top. The correct in-back-to-in arc creates the proper release of the hands and thus the clubhead through the ball.

Hale Irwin

Of all the fine golfers of the modern era Hale Irwin must be close to unique in having never needed a teacher or coach to keep his good looking, sound golf swing in perfect working order.

Hale knew his swing better than anyone and thus would have been mindful of his tendencies. He turned his shoulders very correctly, but occasionally the club follows the body too closely for comfort, which means the hands and arms finish the backswing a fraction flat. From there his hands and arms are inclined to start down a little bit locked together which means Hale is slightly over the top as he starts his downswing and thus the club is slightly outside the line.

I remember one occasion in the mid-1980s, I'd flown out to one of my golf schools in the States and on my arrival I discovered that Hale had been practising at the club for two whole weeks, hitting balls for six hours a day, and not once did he hit a shot other than with his feet together. Bear in mind this is a multiple US Open champion and at that time one of the best players in the world, yet he didn't once hit a regular full shot. That's patience for you. Why did he do it? Well, I'll explain and also tell you why it can be such a wonderful exercise.

One of the most common mistakes among club golfers is they finish the backswing with their shoulders, which makes them swing too flat, and start the downswing with their shoulders, which throws the club away from the body and outside the ideal swing plane. In simple terms, they apply the body too much, too early in the downswing. Hale occasionally suffered from a mild case of this problem.

For anyone who shares this tendency, hitting shots from a very narrow stance is perfect medicine because it encourages you to swing the club down as opposed to swinging yourself. It gets the hands and arms working and promotes a much freer swish of the club down and through. If you start to drift back into old habits and apply too much body action from the top, you very quickly lose your balance.

Next time you're at the range, hit a mid-iron shot with your feet close together. If you lose your balance in the downswing, that's a sign you're applying too much body action. So, get your feet together and point the club at the target at the top of your backswing. As you change direction, feel that your hands and arms start down first and that the body stays 'quiet'.

Finally, a word about the mental side of the game. Think back to the tiny putt that Hale missed in the 1983

Open Championship at Birkdale. Learn from the way he dealt with that. Some golfers would have disappeared without a trace. But Hale kept his composure, went on to shoot a level par 72 that day, and followed it up with a 67 in the final round to put himself right in the frame.

Tom Watson denied him with a brilliant and composed finish, but the point is, Hale was in there with a chance of winning. When things go wrong for you in a competition – say, you get a bad bounce or you make what seems like a stupid mistake – don't let it ruin your entire round. Learn to put it behind you and get on with the game. The next shot is the only shot that matters. It's easier said than done, of course. But I believe if you work at it you can develop a better temperament on the golf course and that can only be of benefit to your scores.

Bobby Jones

Winner of three Opens, four US Opens, one British Amateur and five US Amateurs – all before he reached the age of 30. And he wasn't even playing for money. No wonder some say that Bobby Jones was the greatest golfer of all time.

Some of my earliest memories are of my father talking about the remarkable exploits of Bobby Jones. Even after I had started playing the game, when Henry Cotton had become very much the man of the moment, people would still speak in awe and admiration of the great Bobby Jones. Indeed, many a year would have to pass before people stopped saying to any talented youngster who started to show promise: 'Now then young man, are you going to be another Bob Jones?'

I've watched his classic video tapes dozens of times and marvelled at his gorgeous, rounded, fluent, long golf swing. It was quite rapid by any standards, but the wonderful rhythm and exquisite timing made a metronome look out of kilter. Add this to a sublime and sensitive touch on the greens, using his famous Calamity Jane putter, and one can start to appreciate how great Bobby Jones was.

In 1930 Jones exceeded even his own remarkable standards, winning the British Amateur Championship, the Open Championship, the US Open, and the US Amateur Championship – the Impregnable Quadrilateral as it was dubbed by one New York journalist. He was just 28 years old and, in surely the greatest ever example of quitting while one is ahead, retired from competitive golf.

Returning again to his swing, he had such a confident, letting-go action. By that, I mean the clubhead really free wheeled through the ball. Indeed, I remember reading in one of Jones's books that he felt the clubhead reached maximum speed prior to impact, then freewheeled into the back of the ball. I must say, I like the sound of that – it seemed to me to conjure up the sort of freedom of movement in the downswing that many club golfers could aspire to. More of a swing than a hit, if you like.

Much of this technique could be attributed to the young Bobby Jones watching and, probably to a degree modelling himself on, Stuart Maiden, a Scottish born professional who had emigrated to Atlanta and become the head pro at Jones's home club at East Lake. He later became Jones's teacher and used to travel the world with him. Maiden taught Jones as simply as possible, saying that: 'I knew it was a mistake to confuse him with too many things.' Actually, Jones knew a great deal about the golf swing and later wrote brilliantly about every facet of the game, but Maiden's teaching style obviously worked for him.

If Jones had a fault, it was that the ball forever kept creeping back in his stance. Always conscious of this, Maiden used to say to him in his own charming way: 'Now Mr Jones, ball forward in your stance a bit, please. Come on, just a bit more than that'. He had to gently coax him into the correct position, because Jones used to feel comfortable with the ball too far back in his stance. Most of us are the same. The ball feels best when it's in the middle of our stance because we feel we can hit it from there . . . but we can't hit it straight from there. We tend to push it or hook it. It is one example of why comfortable isn't always correct.

The golfers who should really keep an eye out for this fault are those who tend to hook the ball, because this type of shot pattern is invariably caused by the ball being too far back in the stance. As I've said, it feels comfortable, but the problem is caused because the clubhead meets the ball before it has reached the on-line portion of its swing. It's travelling in-to-out, so you invariably hit it right or with a big hook.

Slicers will have the opposite problem. Their tendency will be to let the ball creep too far forward in the stance, which means the clubhead has travelled beyond the on-line portion of its swing and is thus swinging to the left of target at impact. That's where the pull or the big slice originates.

So how can you take something from the great Bobby Jones and use it to the benefit of your own game? Well, get someone to study your ball position with the driver; it should be opposite the left heel. If it is incorrectly positioned, you need to be coaxed into the correct position. Do please bear in mind, however, that changing ball position is one of those things that takes some doing. Don't immediately expect it to feel right and comfortable; it won't. As I often say to pupils, improving your golf swing involves putting up with a bit of discomfort, because if you change anything meaningful, that is how the first few shots will feel. As long as you remember that it is far more important to be correct than it is to be comfortable, you will always stand a chance of fulfilling your potential.

CHAPTER 9

Playing The Game

Situation: Driving with trouble on the right.

Suggestions: Unless you consistently curve your shots slightly to the left with the driver, this is a good time to consider leaving it in the bag. Two ballistic factors favour using a 3-wood or 4-wood instead in this situation.

First, these clubs are more lofted and shallower-faced than the driver. Thus they usually make contact lower on the back of the ball. The lower contact adds backspin and lessens sidespin. This reduces the degree that the ball will slice into trouble on the right, if you should happen to hit it with an open clubface.

Second, bear in mind that if you should happen to make contact with the clubface closed to the left, the club will be carrying a reduced degree of effective loft. Thus the more lofted 3-wood or 4-wood would be more likely to fly the ball a suitable height than would the straight-faced driver, which might fail to put the ball into the air at all.

The golfer who slices almost all long shots would surely choose a more-lofted club in this situation. He would also be wise to grip the club with his hands turned a little more to the right. This will make it easier for him to square the clubface at impact.

For many golfers it also helps to tee the ball a bit higher than normal in this situation. The higher the ball sits, the more we tend to sweep it away with a somewhat flatter swing. This, in itself, generally squares the clubface a bit sooner in the hitting area.

Situation: Driving on a hole that has trouble down the left.

Suggestions: This situation should not be particularly bothersome for the golfer who invariably slices his drives to the right. With trouble on the left, this is his safest shot.

To further guarantee the slice, however, he might well choose a driver rather than a more lofted club, if he happens to be in doubt about club selection. Because the driver has less loft and a deeper face it tends to contact the ball higher on its backside. This higher contact decreases backspin. Thus any slice spin applied will make the ball curve to the right a greater degree.

The golfer who tends to curve his drives to the left will find it helps to tee the ball a bit lower than normal in this situation. With the ball sitting lower to the ground, he will be less likely to sweep it away with a relatively flat swing, which tends to close the clubface to the left prematurely in the hitting area. Instead, he will instinctively swing on a slightly more upright plane, which tends to delay the squaring of the clubface.

This golfer will also find that a tighter left-hand grip will further reduce any hooking tendency, which in this situation could prove disastrous.

Situation: Playing in a left-to-right crosswind.

Suggestions: Most right-handed golfers hit their worst shots when the wind is blowing from left-to-right. They sense that they must start the shot out to the left to offset the wind. This causes them to swing the club back to the ball from *outside* the target line while – bearing in mind that we stand to the side of the ball – the ideal path is from the *inside*.

Also, the out-to-in path creates a steeply downward angle of approach. This not only reduces distance, because the blow is downward rather than forward, but it also inhibits free swinging of the arms and hands, for fear of burying the clubhead into the ground. This lack of free swinging impedes squaring of the clubface; at impact it still faces to the right, in the direction that the wind is blowing.

Thus it is best to avoid the instinctive temptation to swing the club to the left of where you are aiming – out-to-in – when playing in a left-to-right wind. There are better ways to handle this type of wind. The method you choose, however, should depend on the shot you happen to be playing.

For instance, on a tee shot where you want maximum distance, I suggest, given a wide fairway, you merely play a straight shot down the left side, with the club swinging back to the ball from the *inside*, and allow the wind to curve it back to the centre of the fairway. Since the ball will be curving in the same direction as the wind is blowing, this method will give you good distance.

If, however, the fairway is too narrow to allow the ball to drift to the right with the wind, you will need to play a shot that would normally curve slightly to the left. The wind will offset this normal curve and hold the shot more or less on a straight line.

To play this shot you will need to hit the ball with the clubface turned slightly to the left of your swing path. Since closing the clubface takes loft off the club, I suggest you choose a 3-wood rather than a driver for this shot. The relatively straight-faced driver, when closed, doesn't carry enough loft to give the shot sufficient height. However, the 3-wood when closed becomes, in effect, a 2-wood or a driver. It will give your shot a trajectory that is more or less normal.

To hit the shot with a slightly closed clubface, grip the 3-wood with your hands turned a bit farther to the right than normal. Aim and swing for a straight shot, ignoring the wind.

When hitting approach shots to the green in a left-to-right wind, you again have the same two options. You can either aim to the left and let the wind bring the ball into the flagstick, or you can aim on target and hit a shot that would normally curve to the left, one that will fight the wind and thus stop quickly.

On long approach shots with, say, a 2, 3 or 4-iron, the first option is best. Any attempt to hit these relatively straight-faced irons with a closed clubface would probably leave you with too little effective loft to give the shot sufficient height. Therefore, aim left of target, play a straight shot and let the wind bring it in. The ball will probably bound freely forward and to the right upon landing, however, so plan to land it short of the green and somewhat to the left.

On occasion you may also use this method on shorter approach shots with the more-lofted irons. These shots will fly higher, of course, so you can try to land the ball on the green, left and short of the flagstick, but only if the green is very soft and the flagstick is near the back. Otherwise this plan of action would be dangerous. The ball will be curving from the left, thus flying more or less with the wind. It may not hold the putting surface.

Therefore, as a general rule I suggest that you apply your second option when approaching with a more-lofted iron club in the left-to-right wind. Play the shot that would normally curve left but, because of the counteracting wind, will tend to hold its line. This shot will settle softly on most greens.

To play this shot I suggest you choose a club with more loft than you would normally use for the distance at hand, say an 8-iron instead of a 7-iron, or a 7-iron instead of a 6-iron. With less club in hand, you will need to swing full-out, giving the shot an especially forceful lash with your arms and hands. This extra effort will tend to close the clubface slightly at impact so that the ball can fight the wind and thus hold its line.

You would not want to use this method if you have found that swinging with extra arm and hand action makes you mishit your shots. In that case I suggest you choose the club that you would normally use for the approach shot in question, but make the same grip adjustment that I suggested for tee shots when fighting the left-to-right wind with a 3-wood.

Situation: Playing in a right-to-left crosswind.
Suggestions: The right-handed golfer who normally makes the mistake of swinging on an out-to-in clubhead path will hit some of his best shots when the wind is blowing from

right to left. He senses that he needs to start the ball right to offset the wind. Thus he swings the club into the ball from inside as opposed to his normal out-to-in approach.

When the clubhead's path is from the inside rather than the outside, it's angle of approach is shallower. This sends the force of the blow forward, rather than downward, so the shot travels farther. The path from the inside also encourages a free release of the arms and hands into the shot. This tends to square the clubface on target at impact, rather than leave it open to the right.

When driving down an open fairway in a right-to-left wind, I suggest you merely play a normal drive down the right side of the fairway. Let the wind bring it into the centre of the fairway. The ball will travel good distance because it will be curving in somewhat the same direction as the wind is blowing.

If the fairway is too narrow to allow the ball to drift to the left, you will need to play a drive that would normally curve to the right. The right-to-left wind will disallow much of this curve and thus hold the ball more or less on line. This shot should be simple for golfers whose drives normally curve to the right. Others should grip the club with their hands turned a little farther to the left than normal. This grip will delay the squaring of the clubface so that it still faces slightly to the right at impact, to counteract the right-to-left wind.

Teeing the ball lower than normal has this same counteracting effect. With the ball setting close to the ground we tend to swing more steeply downward to it, to avoid the ground behind it. The steeper angle of approach, in turn, tends to leave the clubface slightly open at impact.

When approaching the green in a right-to-left wind, it

is also best to hit a shot that would normally curve to the right. Again, the wind will hold the ball on line. Since the ball is more or less fighting the wind, it will also settle more quickly on landing, whereas the shot that is allowed to drift to the left, with the wind, will not.

On these approach shots I suggest you choose more club than you would normally use for the distance in questions – a 7-iron rather than an 8-iron, or a 6-iron instead of 7-iron. Knowing that you have too much club in hand, you will instinctively swing with less force than normal. The less-forceful swing will tend to leave the club-face slightly open to the right at impact. This puts a certain amount of left-to-right spin on the ball to offset the right-to-left wind.

Please bear in mind, however, that it is most difficult to apply slice spin to the ball with the more-lofted irons, such as the wedges and 9-iron. These lofted clubs contact the ball so low on its underside that in a large part backspin, rather than slice spin, is applied.

The art of competing

Sir Michael Bonallack, five-times British Amateur champion (and later secretary of the R&A) is the perfect example of what I would call a 'mental golfer'. Perhaps we could say, without being too uncomplimentary, that he is a manoeuvrer; a better competitor than striker. But, of course, that doesn't mean a hoot; the score counts. And when something clicks and he starts to strike the ball well, he wins everything.

Bonallack's best asset, like a lot of great players, is his golfing brain. It has been true of Peter Thomson, Bobby

Locke, Walter Hagen, and many other great golfers. They were good strikers most of the time, perhaps, but their chief asset was a golfing brain which enabled them to overcome mechanical or technical deficiencies. In other words, they could nearly always score well when playing badly. They could *compete*.

I wish more people had this sort of golfing brain. There are no end of golfers who can hit the ball very well, professionals and amateurs alike, but there seem to be very few who can win championships. Those who do are the people who can think properly and keep their cool under heavy pressure.

All tournament players have been in the position many times of coming in after an event having played rubbish. With nine holes to go they have more or less given up mentally, and tended to play sloppily as a result. Then, once in, they have found they lost by a shot or two. You always imagine that other people are doing far better than you are. Club golfers will have experienced the same thing.

This is a problem inherent in every form of competition where the action is spread out. The only answer is confidence in oneself, and a relentless determination to keep trying whatever happens. Perhaps a 'big head' helps; the sort of attitude that no one can do better than you in the long run. Mind you, there is no need to tell everyone that!

Just how do you score well when playing badly? Especially when you have been playing well and the collapse is sudden and shocking.

The most vital thing is to know what you can fall back on simply to move the ball from A to B, a reliable shot which comes to you easily, under any sort of pressure. I think this is the most important single piece of armament in a good golfer's arsenal. It doesn't matter if the shot is a slice, a hook, or even a half-top, so long as it is repeatable; so long as it can be played with confidence at any time.

Too many good golfers try too hard for technical perfection, and not hard enough to score well while striking poorly. Nobody ever hits every single shot perfectly. Even the finest strikers only hit six or seven shots in any one round exactly as they mean to. Many competent golfers find it difficult to accept this situation. They seek perfect striking and are unduly disappointed and disillusioned by their bad shots, which adversely affects their confidence and tenacity. It is impossible to achieve perfection of strike, even on a practice ground, so how much more difficult must it be when the shots count; when one is playing under pressure?

If a Peter Thomson or a Gary Player went into a championship not hitting the ball well he would be what I'd call 'sensibly perturbed'. He would certainly be looking for 'a way' in his mind and on the practice ground. But he would not be completely demoralised, because of his ability to compete. Whereas a lot of people in this position would be beaten before they even left the 1st tee. They would panic and become demoralised. The great competitor knows that he is a *pretty good striker*, which is all you need to be to win a great deal if you have the right mental attitude. If you haven't got the right mental attitude, you need to be a superlative striker to finish anywhere in the running. It would seem to me that the good competitor will go on winning almost irrespective of his striking, whereas the good striker who is a poor competitor is likely to shine only occasionally.

A bad start will quickly kill off the majority of golfers –

sap both their confidence and their desire. I once asked one of the finest competitors in tournament golf what his reaction would be to starting a major championship with a seven: 'I would just try to forget the seven and go on playing the other holes as they came. I certainly wouldn't be trying to make a sudden, dramatic recovery. I wouldn't think 'now I've got to go 3-3-3,' or anything like that. You can never expect too much too fast. Over-anxiety to recoup a shot too often leads to loss of more. You have to wait for it, wait for the opportunities.

'I like to start off quietly. I don't believe in attacking right from the gun. The same applies with putting. I'll be happy to get down in two. Once I've got the mood of the game and am getting into it, then I feel like I can start attacking. Even when you have 'played yourself in' there will be days when you are striking the shots well but the score won't come. There is absolutely no percentage in getting distressed about it, as many golfers do. You can only go on trying to do your best and wait.'

Whatever your level, remember that – with the right effort – you can almost always score better than you played. The word for it is *competing*.

Attitude

There is no doubt in my mind that lower scores will come about from improving both your impact conditions and your understanding of various on-course situations. I am equally certain, however, that almost all weekend golfers also need an improved attitude before they will ever play to their true potential.

Proper attitude in golf is probably a subject that is

worthy of an entire book in itself. Here, however, I will mention three particular characteristics that dramatically separate, say, a Bobby Jones, a Ben Hogan, a Henry Cotton or a Bobby Locke from the average weekend player.

First, those great players were successful because they realised their limitations. They knew that some shots are all but impossible for anyone to play successfully. They knew that other shots were beyond their own particular abilities. Like great generals, they knew when to charge and when to retreat.

Though far less skilled, most weekend golfers that I have seen seldom retreat. I see them attempt shots that are doomed to fail in themselves, apart from the additional wasted strokes that they bring about. So learn to play within your limitations and attempt only those shots that you can reasonably expect to achieve, even if they might not be all that spectacular. Sometimes it's far better to accept the loss of one stroke instead of risking total disaster.

Second, you should work on developing the positive approach that is far more common among great players than among weekend golfers. Try to maintain the same attitude and degree of concentration that you adopt when you are two down with four holes to play. Avoid the negative thinking that comes when we are two up with four to go, or when we've just finished the front nine with a good score, the attitude that says: 'I've got to be careful that I don't ruin everything with this one shot.'

Finally, *try on every shot*. We are all determined to do our best on the first tee. We continue in this vein until disaster strikes, as it invariably does sooner or later. Then, so often, comes the blow-up.

Continuing with your best effort after running into trouble – and succeeding as a result – is surely the best way to get maximum satisfaction from playing golf. Come to think of it, the same would hold true of life itself.

Follow Jack's methodical approach

I have found certain ways to make my actual practice time more productive. It is all too true in golf that lots of practice, if misspent, will not produce any improvement.

To make our practising more productive, we could all benefit from the example set by Jack Nicklaus. I have never seen Jack hit a practice shot without first giving it the same careful thought that he would apply in a key competitive situation.

Without fail he plans the shot and his execution of it before he ever steps up to the ball. He is particularly careful to aim the club and address the ball correctly, as you should be. I suspect that this care taken in practice is a major reason why Jack competes so well under pressure. His routine on the course is the same as he has applied countless times in practice. The weekend golfer who does not practise as he plays feels lost to a certain degree on many shots that he must play on the course.

There is, however, one difference between the way you should practise and the way you should play. I suggest that you limit yourself in practice to no more than two thoughts during each swing. I suggest you limit yourself on the course to only one such thought. I would remind you to go through your address procedure on every shot prior to swinging.

I also believe that every golfer, even the non-practiser,

should hit at least a few shots before each round of play. This is vital, not only for getting the feel of a club in your hands, but also for finding your swing thought for the day. You will score better on average if you never walk on to the first tee without having first decided on the one thing you will think about as you swing the club.

Finally, a word about mastering a new swing technique through practice; select a target that is about 20 yards closer than you would normally expect to hit shots with this club. The reason for doing this is to make yourself swing at a tempo that is slow enough for your brain and body to perform an unfamiliar function. Adults, especially, need to swing at a brain speed that gives them time not only to do what the instructor has suggested, but also to sense – to feel – themselves doing it, so that they can repeat the correct feeling on future shots.

Give it your all

I am not one of those teachers who advocate that a golfer should play within himself using, say, only 80 per cent power, as if anyone of us is capable of making such a measurement. I believe it is easier to hit the ball with as much power as you can muster without losing your balance.

By the same token, when you are between clubs I would normally go for the weaker club and make a full-blooded hit. If you select the club which is strong for the distance, it is vital to grip down the shaft and give the shot the full treatment. Soft or quiet shots using a portion of your power are much more difficult.

When Seve Ballesteros blew his chances in the Masters

with that infamous second shot into the pond on Augusta's 15th hole in 1986, it was clear the moment he made contact that the clubhead was decelerating in the hitting area. Subconsciously he knew that the club he had in his hands was too strong for the distance. In Seve's defence, he was having to wait and watch Jack Nicklaus going mad, making an eagle, in front of him.

By contrast, when Jose Maria Olazabal was in a similar position on that hole in the 1994 Masters he selected a club which needed to be hit 100 percent perfectly and with all his power in order to carry to the green.

Of course, this doctrine requires that the player has a realistic idea of how far he hits each club. Regrettably, most club golfers kid themselves about their power.

A waste of my time and your money

Regrettably too many lessons do not do a scrap of good. I have reached this bleak conclusion after many years of trying to help golfers who come to me with deeply ingrained bad habits. With this type of pupil it is easy enough to get them hitting shots which are an absolute revelation. I can show them their potential for hitting shots which are beyond their wildest ambitions. But bad habits die hard and unless the pupil is prepared to work long and hard on the practice ground the bad habit will reassert itself.

These days when, for example, an habitual slicer seeks help I often start by asking how much time and effort he is prepared to put into the physiotherapy exercises after I have rebroken the bone of his bad habit and set it straight. If he says that he really cannot spare the time to practice much, which is the case for many people, I tell him: 'Then go on the way you are now and simply aim off to allow for your slice.'

Golf with the nerve removed

Hitting a few balls into a net may be all very well to loosen up before play, but extended practice sessions in the net can be dangerous. I had a low-handicap friend who went skiing in Switzerland every winter and in order to keep his golf swing in trim he went to one of the golf schools in Crans sur Sierre in the evenings and hit buckets of balls into a net. When he returned to our Sandy Lodge club he had the biggest hook you ever saw.

In a net you have none of the fears you encounter on the course, such as woods and rough and ponds and out-of-bounds. So you swing easily and the tendency is to hit harder and harder and sometimes for the grip to get stronger and stronger. You need to see the flight of the ball when you practise so that you can detect a fault and remedy it before it develops into a full-blown habit.

Kid yourself

When a golfer is two up with four to play he is tempted to overdo the safety first policy. He takes what he believes to be extra care on every stroke and steers well clear of any possible danger. All too often this pussyfooting costs him the match. In this situation try to imagine that you are two down with four to play and suit your tactics accordingly. It helps me. Sometimes.

In a world of slicers, the hooker is king

Most of the great players are fighting a hook. So in their ghost written instruction articles for the golf magazines they tend to advocate a weaker grip than normal, that is with both hands rotated anticlockwise combined with a late hit.

The effect of this expert anti-hook instruction being disseminated to a world of slicers can be easily imagined. The slicers get worse and flock to me and the other teachers in droves. I'm not complaining, mind. I have always appreciated the time and effort the superstars put in to drum up business for me.

Some of those magazine readers whose fades have been converted into vicious slices by following the wise advice of the star players ask me: 'How do I get a late hit?'

I counter with the stock reply: 'What is wrong with hitting at the right time?' End of discussion.

Let it happen

You play your best golf by letting your swing just happen, not by concentrating on making it happen.

Golf instruction often creates over-control. So the mood of a swing should be to 'set it up' (that is, to take a correct address position), 'set it off' (swing the club up to a position from which you can hit the ball) and 'let it freewheel'.

Safety first

Every good player has a 'safe' shot he can rely on for those occasions when he is facing a particularly narrow fairway, or when the nerves are jangling from the tensions of the moment, or when his regular game is slightly off key. It is invariably a fade, maybe not as long as a normal drive and not so spectacular – but safe.

Tee the ball low. This helps a fade; a high tee tends to promote a hook through hitting early with the hands and rolling the wrists over. Set up open to the ball aiming up the left-hand side of the fairway. Open the clubface and hold it open going through the ball, keeping the hands ahead of the clubhead. Make sure you turn through as you hit the ball, obviating any independent hand action.

Play your percentages

Although when we practise we aim for perfection, even Ben Hogan when he played a record-breaking round reckoned that he hit no more than four or five shots which satisfied 100 percent. Golf is a game of misses and the way to win competitions is to hit all your shots with only as much of your power potential as allows you to swing in balance.

Practice swings

Golfers frequently remark: 'If only I could hit the ball with my practice swing.' For purposes of discussion, let us assume that the speaker really does have the perfect practice swing to which he lays claim. It would do him no good to hit the ball with it.

A golf swing is only as good as the position of the club-face at impact. The arc of the swing may be perfect, but if the clubface of the driver is more than three degrees off square we miss the fairway. A practice swing is therefore devoid of fear since the squareness (or otherwise) of the clubface at impact is of no account. There is no impact and therefore there is no apprehension.

Never give up

Early in my career I was playing in a competition and soon into the round I suffered a disaster that cost me four or five strokes. It was a real body blow and completely knocked the stuffing out of me, to the extent that for the rest of the round I was just going through the motions. I stopped competing and, my goodness, how the strokes mounted up. In retrospect that was not such a disaster because it taught me a valuable lesson. As Bobby Jones remarked with his customary sagacity: you learn only from your mistakes.

When I am trying to impress on professional golfers the importance of trying your utmost on every shot I remind them that almost always the winner will have had at least two disasters in his four rounds.

The most salutary example I ever witnessed of the virtue of trying on every shot was Jack Nicklaus in the first round of the Open Championship at Sandwich in 1981. On the eve of the championship he had received word of his son Stevie's car accident and with his mind in a turmoil of worry he was hitting the ball very badly by his standards in the dreadful conditions of wind and rain in that opening round.

I had gone back to my hotel and watched, in fascination, the drama on TV. He was on the 13th hole and at that point was about 12 over par. But he was not giving up; he was obviously trying his very hardest on every stroke and scrambling magnificently. I think he got up and down four times to restrict his score to 83.

The next day, after reassuring news from home, he played a fine round of 66 and just made the cut, which he would not have done if he had packed it in the previous day. That was a wonderful lesson from the greatest competitor there has ever been.

Attitude of the man maketh the golfer

The great Walter Hagen was truly the king of matchplay – he did, after all, win five US PGA Championships at a time when that was a matchplay event. Obviously he was no fool when it came to strokeplay. But somehow, head-to-head combat brought out the best in him. Much of this success would have to be attributed to his totally unflappable nature. Bobby Jones, who suffered his worst ever defeat at the hands of Hagen – an 11&10 drubbing over four rounds – said that it was a joy to play with him. 'He goes along chin up,' Jones described, 'smiling away, never grousing about his luck, playing the ball as he finds it.'

This is one of the reasons why matchplay agreed with Hagen. He refused to let anything get to him. If he hit a bad shot, it was done, history – there was nothing he could do about it. By shrugging it off he stayed relaxed, yet mentally sharp, and thus better equipped to make sure the next shot was a good one.

Hagen's 'smell the flowers' attitude is an example to us

all. If you can learn to keep your composure after the bad shots, I guarantee you'll hit fewer of them. Byron Nelson was one golfer who learnt the importance of staying cool. Early in his career he got so angry during one tournament that he threw his putter up a tree, which as you can imagine wouldn't have done his score a power of good. He vowed from thereon never to let his temper get the better of him, forcing himself to breathe more slowly and even walk slowly in potentially stressful situations.

Whether you choose to smell the flowers as Hagen did, or breathe slowly like Nelson, it's entirely up to you. What is important is that you find a way, any way, of staying calm on the golf course. Because the minute you lose your cool, you stop thinking clearly. And that's when you make big mistakes.

On a personal note, when I played in the 1950s and early 1960s I occasionally became very annoyed with myself. If I was playing today I would enlist the help of a sports psychologist, as do many of today's golfers.

Mental pictures must come first

The golfer with an effective short game, the man or woman who can consistently lay those little pitch and chip shots close enough to the hole for a single putt, really does have a tremendous advantage. Confidence in one's short game gives a tremendous edge at all levels of competition.

The sad thing is that so few people command a sound short game when, whatever their standard with the long shots, it is well within their reach. Here is the area of the game where the fellow who booms the ball 300 yards off the tee is pulled back to equal terms with the chap who

can never manage more than 210 yards. This is the department of the game that calls for nothing more than good
mental imagery and 'touch'.

The techniques for pitching and chipping are simple,
but before getting into them I want to stress this imagery
factor. As I have stressed before in this book, you should
never play a short shot until you have a clear mental
picture of how you want the ball to behave.

This really is the secret of a strong short game. Until
you decide how far and high the ball should fly, where
it should land and how much it should roll, you cannot
select the right club for the job. And what prevents so
many people from developing a good short game is their
illogical use of the same favourite club for every shot.
There is no way that one club will get the ball close to the
hole in every situation when you miss a green.

By using the wrong club for the particular shot at hand,
you introduce a needless variable. If you choose a club with
too much loft for a little chip from the fringe, in some way
you will have to deloft it during the stroke. Conversely,
if you choose a too-straight faced club, there will be a
tendency to scoop at the ball to get it into the air. Selection
of the correct club will allow you to play the same, simple
stroke under all circumstances, with the club's loft automatically governing flight and roll.

Watch the extreme care with which the pros think out
and plan these little shots in tournaments and you will get
an idea of how important it is to 'picture' the shot, then
select the club that will match the picture.

Beating the weather

Brute strength and blind fury will achieve even less in bad weather than in perfect playing conditions. When you are cold, stiff-muscled, or restricted by clothing, any effort to smash the cover off the ball leads generally to an even greater loss of control. To know not only what you are trying to do, but what you are capable of doing, is always a help at golf. In rough weather it is essential. You must be prepared to play more conservatively, and when a birdie does come along, slip it on to your score as a pleasant surprise rather than an anticipated bonus.

Do not force the long par-4s and 5s. Accept the fact that in winter a long par-4 may become a par-5, and a reachable par-5 in summer a much more difficult five. Give yourself plenty of club, and accept the conditions as you find them. Never try to bash the ball into submission. The quickest way to fall flat on your face in bad weather is to try to tear the course apart.

The chief technical problem in wet conditions is to strike the ball squarely and cleanly. Water, mud and long wet grass combine against you to make this extremely difficult. Consequently, it is worth sacrificing a little distance in favour of a more solid strike. Think 'strike it flush', not 'hit it far'. Quiet your game down, if necessary, in order to swing the clubface squarely into the back of the ball.

Generally in bad weather or ground conditions you should use more loft than you would normally. You need to get a wet ball flying, so don't overdo the straight-faced clubs. The 4 and 5-woods can effectively replace the 2, 3 and 4-irons, especially among poorer players. These lofted woods will move the ball well even from wet rough, and are a boon for long shots from soggy or 'shaggy' fairways.

Possibly the worst of all rough weather problems is wind. This is really what plays havoc with our enjoyment and our scores.

The answer, again, is to keep your head; to accept the added difficulties and to counter them by playing within yourself. The wind should be used rather than fought. When you are playing against it, take plenty of club, *really* over-club, shorten and slow down your back-swing, keep your feet on the ground, and endeavour to swing the clubhead not *at* but *through* the ball.

Too many golfers, even good ones, cannot make them-selves punch say a low 5-iron when the distance in normal conditions would require a 7-iron. They would rather gamble on hitting a 'miracle' 7-iron. Of course, 99 times out of 100 such a shot will be blown away, but these stalwarts never learn. They seem to feel that they can allow themselves to attempt only the shots that they regard as 'proper shots'. I can assure them that *any* shot arriving on target, no matter how it got there, is an excellent shot in a pro's book.

Downwind the ball will fly farther, so long as you give it plenty of air. Adjust your club selection accordingly. Very often, in a strong backwind, a 3-wood from the tee will go farther through the air than a driver, but will stop quicker. Make use of this sort of knowledge when the conditions are against you.

High crosswinds are everybody's nightmare, but again, they can be used rather than fought. My tactics vary according to the distance of the shot and the degree of accuracy needed. In a big right-to-left wind, I would aim off to the right on the tee and let the wind bring the ball back into the centre of the fairway. In the same wind on an approach shot I would probably try to cut the ball into the wind, hold it up by shaping it into the wind, because a with-the-wind hooked shot is difficult to control when the target is small.

This, of course, demands a high level of ball control, which many golfers don't pretend to possess. Even so, they must decide how their standard shot is likely to be affected by wind, and make an appropriate allowance in aim.

The essential thing is to decide very clearly what you are trying to do before you actually attempt it.

Aim high

Unless ground conditions are very dry, hit your full 7, 8, and 9-irons not at the hole but at the top of the flag. These are the scoring clubs. Use them as such. Most handicap golfers are prone to under-club on approach shots. Instead of, say, hitting a controlled 7-iron at the stick, they thrash an 8-iron at the green. I find I tend to do this when I'm not playing well, but if I'm hitting the ball solidly I take ample club and fire straight at the top of the stick.

Most handicap players are often surprised at the clubs the best players use in approaching. Sam Snead, for instance, would often use a 7-iron where most players would try to wallop an 8-iron. You don't get prizes for distance with the pitching clubs. A controlled shot at the flag is always a much higher percentage than a big, swinging thrash in the general direction of the green.

From good to great

It says a lot about the inner drive of the true champions that even when they are enjoying great success, making pots of money and winning tournaments, they are prepared to jump off the gravy train and work for months on end to improve their technique.

The first example that comes to mind is Byron Nelson. I first met him in 1955 when I played in the old Thunderbird Classic and he invited me to join him in a practice round. What a player! He made me feel like a 15-handicapper. I did not have an opportunity to talk with him again until 1967 when we were both doing television commentaries on the Open Championship at Hoylake.

I used positively to devour instruction books in those days, any golf books come to that, and I had read his book. So I commented that when he started out he must have swung the club in a very flat arc. He made that flat swing work well enough to win tournaments but he was not consistent. He would win a tournament and the next week he would fail to qualify. So he took three months off and changed his grip, removing two of his three knuckles from view, and working on taking the club straight back and up.

Having grooved his adjusted swing he made a statement that, for a man of such inherent humility, bordered on providence-tempting arrogance: 'I believed I would never play badly again.' But that was about the size of it. He never did.

In his first instruction book, *Power Golf,* Ben Hogan advocated a three-knuckle grip and that is how he played. In my conversation with Nelson I remarked that it had taken a serious car accident to force Hogan to change his grip. Nelson corrected me. He said that Hogan had been practising with a weak left-hand grip before the accident – Henry Cotton said that it was he who had convinced Hogan of the need for such a change – but that when he got out on the course Hogan reverted to his familiar three-knuckle grip.

Having read *Power Golf* I had been very anxious to watch Hogan and I had my opportunity at the 1953 Open Championship at Carnoustie. His grip was completely different from the illustrations in the book. Hogan's enforced layoff produced what was probably the most thorough and effective revision of a golf swing of them all.

Roberto de Vicenzo, that lovely self-deprecating character with his infectious good humour and fractured English, was another player who realised that he could never achieve his full potential until he eliminated a fault. His left hand was too far over the top of the club and it took him six months, hitting a thousand balls a day, to get comfortable with his new grip. Then he won the Open Championship and almost won the Masters.

Nick Faldo is a recent example of a highly successful player withdrawing from competitive play to rebuild his swing. He was a 'rocker' and he was very fortunate to find in David Leadbetter a teacher so well suited to his needs. It seems to me that Faldo sees golf in terms of infinite complexity whereas I believe and teach that golf, although admittedly a most difficult game, is essentially a simple game. Indeed I might go as far to say the simpler the better.

Jack Nicklaus never actually withdrew from competitive golf in order to make changes to his swing. But he was a prodigious worker on his golf. He established what is now the standard routine for professional golfers of hitting hundreds of balls a day and also of going straight to the practice ground after a competitive round in order to iron out a fault. For years he struggled, without lasting success, to convert his shoulder tilt into a turn.

One day when I was in his office I was emboldened to remark, using the verbal shorthand of the profession: 'You won most of your titles missing it.' He grinned and replied: 'Yes, but I'm smarter than the other guys.' And that was no less than the truth of it.

Mix in the best company you can find

Mix with and try to play with better golfers than yourself. Most good golfers are only too glad to encourage others to play the game well, and, once the ice is broken, can be of great help in doing so. This is not a question of learning to swing. It is more a question of learning scoring technique, strategy, tactics, when to pitch, when to chip, how to recover from trouble, when to play safe and when to attack, and so on. Careful observation of the good player in these areas can be very instructive – as, too, is the effect on one's own game of watching a good method and witnessing a good score.

Four final thoughts to help you play your best

The more I teach, play and watch golf, the more convinced I become that the decisive factor in good shot-making is preparation: shot assessment, club selection, grip, aim, stance, posture. If you can master these departments you have every chance of playing golf to the best of your capabilities, whatever those may be. These are the spade-work areas; the foundations upon which your game must be built if you have the ambition and the opportunity to reach your full potential as a golfer. Of that I am totally convinced, and I am sure I would be supported in this view by the majority of the world's top players.

But there are a few other aspects of the game that I want to mention before we close, which golfers of all calibre tend to overlook or forget.

First of all, I would like to ask you always to remember with what you hit a golf ball. It is not your shoulder pivot, your straight left arm, your bent right arm, your knees, your hips, nor even your hands. It is *the head of the golf club*. In the last analysis, what golf is all about is apply-ing the head of the club to the ball as fast and as flush as possible.

Now, this might sound rather an elementary point to labour, but I feel that it is increasingly overlooked these days, especially by beginners. We live in an age of applied science, to which golf has become subject perhaps more than any other sport. It is such a difficult game to play very well, and so many millions of people now want to do so, that 'method' has become almost a religion. Even though I teach individuals, rather than a 'method', I wouldn't argue with that. It is fun, if you are keen on something, to immerse yourself in the theory of it; and, so long as you are discerning and selective, it is often possible to pick up something of value.

But do not let theoretical 'method' blind you to the basic objective of the game, which is to propel the ball forward with the club, not with some part or the whole of your anatomy. In short, whatever simple or complicated manoeuvres the search for better shots leads you into, don't ever forget to include among them swinging the clubhead into the ball.

This is especially true if you are a slicer, which 80 per cent of golfers are naturally. In the simplest terms, you never get the clubhead to the ball before you are past it with your body – you never hit 'early enough' *with the club*. If you want the fastest cure I know, simply hit shots with your feet together – and I mean *together*. That way you can only do the job with the clubhead. If you don't you will fall over!

The second thought I would like to leave with you concerns your own physical limitations. It is not easy to assess realistically and then candidly accept one's inadequacies, but doing so is a particularly essential operation for the golfer, because the game he plays is not one of power, but power under control.

Nine out of ten pupils who come to me want to hit the ball farther. Very often I can help them, by showing them how to hit it accurately and solidly with an easy swing, instead of approximately and glancingly with a difficult or furious one. But what I cannot do – nor can any other teacher – is increase their natural clubhead speed. Everyone has a definite point, depending on natural muscularity, coordination and playing experience, where he can equate speed (or power) with control. He should find it then play always within it if the score is more important than the exercise. This is a lesson that every successful golfer learned early and has stuck to. You will never meet a top tournament pro who swings as hard as he could physically, other than in exceptional circumstances for an occasional recovery shot.

My third point concerns your attitude on the golf course. Even if you have the ability to hit the most perfect shots in the world, you won't win matches and tournaments unless you can play them strategically and tactically. So, whatever your limitations or advantages as a shot-maker, never forget to apply yourself assiduously to the arts of scoring. Bear in mind that many, many victories have been won, in first-class and club golf, by inferior strikers who could get the ball from A to B, over superb stylists and stroke-makers who couldn't answer the strategic or temperamental problems set by the course and the competitive situation. Remember that golf is a game of how many, not how; that people may often be interested in *what* you scored, but rarely in *how*.

Finally, I would ask you to do what sounds quite a simple thing but is, in fact, very difficult: to try your utmost on every shot. Golf can be the most frustrating and infuriating, as well as the most satisfying and elating, of games; but if it has one cliché that cannot be denied it is that the game is never over until the last putt has been holed.

So, don't give up – ever. Think about what you are trying to do, which is to make a good impact. Think about what will help you to make a good impact, which, to put it as simply as I can, is correct aim and stance followed by two turns, one to get your body out of the way while you aim the club, and one to get it out of the way while you swing the club through the ball. Think out the shots *before* you play them, then think of one key factor to help you swing as you have planned.

There's never been a greater game for triers.

Keeping golf in its right place

Golf being the difficult game that it is, it is very easy for any of us to lose our sense of proportion about it. I seem to meet far too many people who regard as a disaster of the first magnitude a couple of fluffed pitches or a drive into the rough. In point of fact, of course, the greatest players hit very few shots completely as they intend to; and I think it does much for our temperament in golf if we realize and accept this. I often want to say to one of my pupils: 'Who are you to think you can do more than they can!'

If golf is a difficult game, however, we should all be the more grateful for our good shots. After all, the game is tougher than any of us – and will always win. The best players will follow a sparkling 64 with a puzzled 75; or will win a tournament one week – and fail to qualify the next!

Try hard we must – but we must also keep a sense of proportion!

CHAPTER 10

I Had Some Fun Along the Way!

Hit for six

Practice rounds can be terribly slow, and none slower than
the occasion when I was playing in the Open Championship one year with Peter Alliss at St Andrews. We hit putt
after putt on the 5th green while waiting for the 6th fairway to clear, until at last I was able to call him from the
side of the green that it was time to move on. He picked
up my ball and bowled it to me overarm. Responding to
this cricketing motif I swung my putter and by the most
amazing fluke caught the ball absolutely flush. The ball
flew like a bullet and almost decapitated someone on the
12th green.

Having established that nobody had in fact been injured
we played on, but when we finished I was given the dreaded
news that the R&A secretary required my presence in his
office. Forthwith. The formidable Brigadier Brickman duly
gave me a thorough and well-deserved dressing down.
I expressed my sincere regrets and that was that.

He was a man of great charm and, having done his
duty, he switched the conversation to more congenial top-
ics. We soon discovered a mutual and abiding interest in

fishing and cricket and so begun a firm friendship which strengthened and endured until the day he died.

NB. In May 2004 Peter and I were granted honorary life membership of the R&A. We were both so thrilled. What a wonderful journey it's been since that Open Championship at St Andrews so many years ago.

A discreet silence

On the eve of the final against Gary Player in the South African Matchplay Championship we received word that my wife's father had died. Rita took the morning's flight back to London. She was sitting next to three air crew from South African Airways and as the plane approached Nairobi one of them went forward to the flight deck and returned with the dire news: 'That roineck is one up on Gary!' Rita said not a word.

At Athens another enquiry was made of the radio reports and came back with the stupefying news: 'That roineck has beaten Gary on the last green!'

Only now did their travelling companion permit herself the immense pleasure of announcing: 'I am Mrs John Jacobs, the wife of that roineck.'

Physician heal thyself? Not at my age!

When I retired from competitive golf I lost my enthusiasm for my own game and hardly played for many years. I had a living to make and in this was greatly helped by a man who was to become one of the great influences in my life. Laddie Lucas, the left-handed Walker Cup player, was a member at my club, Sandy Lodge in Hertfordshire, and also, of course, a much decorated fighter ace from the war. I had also served in the RAF so we had two strong interests in common, but it was the fact that we got on so well on a personal level that led us into a business partnership.

From that sprang the pioneering idea of formally structured golf centres and the ones we built in Britain and Ireland remain the models for golf centres and schools all over the world. Add writing books and magazine articles, coaching the national teams of ten countries, doing television commentaries, making films and videos, giving private lessons around the world, group instruction, setting up the PGA European Tour and teaching the teachers for the John Jacobs Golf Centres in America – all intensely golf-related activities – and you can see how I became over-golfed without even playing the game.

For relaxation I preferred fly fishing. But in the last five years or so, as I've eased off on my working schedule, I have rediscovered the joys of playing the game. I must confess that in my capacity as a professional golf analyst I cannot give myself high marks for style or performance these days. I experiment and do things I tell others not to do. But I do enjoy it, and that, after all, is the purpose of golf.

Hopeless cases

The only people whose golf cannot be improved are those who won't listen!

Player on Jacobs

In 1986 Gary Player was asked, looking back with all the experience he had gathered in the interim, how he would assess John Jacobs's mark that he has made upon the world game. Player paused for a moment, those big round and strikingly brown eyes staring out in front of him. When he spoke he gave the impression that he wanted his answer to seem important and that he was in earnest about it.

'Plenty of us,' he said, measuring his words, 'enjoy playing golf. It's a wonderful game. It brings lifelong friendships and it takes us to beautiful places. All that is for ourselves. But there are very few in the game who can actually say that they give others enjoyment. John is one of the few. He is a contributor to people's golfing enjoyment – through his teaching, his instructional books, but also his companionship and humour, by his television work and the interest he takes in others, in their golf and in their lives. His input into the game, over all the years I have known him, has been, frankly, exceptional; and he has said very little about it.

'I have seen John in so many roles and circumstances. He has beaten me in competition, and I have beaten him. He has helped me at times with my game when I was in need of a fresh view on my action. And I believe that, now and then in his playing days, maybe I lent him a hand with his. But in all this time, it is really as a contributor – putting more in than ever he could take out for himself – that I mainly remember him. And he always seemed to give the impression of being enthusiastic about it – of *wanting* to do it and not because he had to.'

Player paused again. 'I suppose, when you weigh it all up, the thing with John is that he has put the game and people's enjoyment of it first. That way, he has given them enjoyment – and earned a lot of success for himself.'

Take it easy

You should always practise the full swing with a relatively easy club. I used to wear out 6-irons on the practice ground.

A television director who had just taken up golf asked if I would take a look at his swing. I agreed and when I met him on the practice ground he had a collection of the oldest balls you ever saw and a 2-iron. Obviously he did not hit that 2-iron very well. None of us plays his best golf with a 2-iron.

Later that day while I was doing my television commentary, Brian Barnes fluffed a bunker shot and the ball moved about two feet. I remarked: 'That reminds me of our director's 2-iron.'

A voice in my headphones came back immediately: 'You're fired!'

Booed at St Andrews

The 1955 Open Championship was blessed with balmy sunshine. The Old Course at St Andrews was playing hard and fast, the way a links course should. I had started 70, 71 and, so far as John Jacobs was concerned, God was in His heaven and all was right with the world. I was not so naive as to start anticipating events, but I was doing all right and knew that if I could just keep it going, well . . . who knows what might happen?

My second shot to the 17th green finished on a slight downslope just short of the Road Hole bunker. I surveyed the situation carefully, noting the flag position and scanning how much green I had to work with, assessing the chances of recovery if my ball went over the green on to the road (cobbled in those days, as opposed to the effete Tarmac of today). I allowed myself a quick glance at the sea of hard-eyed, calculating faces of the spectators crowded behind the wall.

The Scots have a well-deserved reputation for being the most discerning golf watchers in the world, and applause sounds much sweeter when it comes from people who can recognise and appreciate the distinction between a standard shot and a good shot. But at times like this, those knowing Scottish galleries can take on the aura of a jury at a murder trial. I knew well enough that if this had been a quiet Saturday evening and I were playing for half a crown with a friend, I could nip the ball right up to the flag. The spectators understood as much, too. But this was the Open Championship and I needed to finish 4, 4 to go into the last round in second place, right in contention, challenging for the Open title.

There was a low, guttural murmuring of disapproval as I set myself to chip in a direction well wide of the line to the flag. The gallery's derisive mumbling at my faint-hearted decision, or what I would prefer to call endorsement of the notion that discretion is the better part of valour, degenerated into outright booing as I clipped the ball up to the front of the green.

I now faced an enormous putt with a deceptively severe right-to-left swing, presenting a risk of putting into the Road Hole bunker. I holed that huge putt – and a detonation of applause from behind the ball signalled the rehabilitation of John Jacobs in the estimation of the world's most knowledgeable crowd.

Eventually there was to be no happy ending. As usual, I came a cropper in the final round, taking seven at the 14th.

Hole in one, just as intended!

The relative exclusiveness of the game of golf in Pakistan in the 1960s was shown by a revealing incident which occurred towards the end of Jacobs's second stay in the country. He had already designed the front nine holes of one of the Peshawar courses on his previous visit. Now he had returned to complete the second half. To help get the feel of it, he was playing holes with the Commander in Chief of the Air Force and two other officers.

Jacobs and his party were about to play their tee shots to the 180-yard 11th hole. Before the gaze of five or six hundred uninitiated spectators, an Englishman, playing with the local professional, shouted across that his pro had just holed the 16th in one. Before hitting his tee shot to the 11th, Jacobs called back: 'If you watch carefully, you will see how it's done.' The 3-iron went straight into the hole! 'The amusing thing,' recalls Jacobs, 'was that most of the spectators who saw the shot, not being golfers, thought that it was intended!'

That same evening, Jacobs was flown by helicopter to Lahore to dine with Ayub Khan, Pakistan's president. It made a good story over dinner. The president, himself a keen golfer, was well aware that 3-irons cannot be made like that to order.

. . . and a couple more aces, to boot

Holes in one have an attraction for Jacobs. Maybe it is because his own 'aces' have occurred in unusual circumstances. There are two more to set beside the strange affair in Pehsawar.

Soon after the Ryder Cup team returned from Palm Springs, Frank Pennink, a highly competent British amateur before the war and, after it, a distinguished golf course architect, rang up Jacobs at Sandy Lodge. Pennink was the writing a weekly golf column for the *Sunday Express* and hit on the idea of playing a round with each member of the team, picking out the particular club with which the player was identified. He asked Jacobs what he might do with him, which was different from the rest:

'I didn't hesitate. There was a very strong wind blowing that day so I said to Frank, "why don't you feature long-iron play into the wind?"'

The two got round to the 15th, a good one-shotter straight into the eye of the wind. 'Here's one to test us today,' commented Jacobs as he prepared to drive a 2-iron at the green, low under the wind. Drilled navel high, straight at the stick, the ball pitched once just short of the flag and rolled slowly into the cup.

But, of all his strange 'aces', perhaps the most bizarre occurred at the short 17th on the New Course at Sunningdale. It was midwinter and Jacobs was playing with the local assistant against two Hunt brothers, Bernard and Geoffrey. The golf, as he remembers it, was exceptionally good:

'There were birdies galore. Pars were of little use. 3s and 2s were the order. My partner and I were beaten 3&2 on the 16th green. I had originally talked Bernard into playing for a fiver, so I said to him on the 17th tee, "come on, £10 or nothing on the bye."'

Hunt accepted the challenge with just a hint of mis-giving. 'All right Jacobs,' he countered, 'but with a nose and a name like yours, you'll probably get a one.'

A few moments later, they were picking Jacobs's 6-iron out of the cup!

Command performances

Before the restoration of the Spanish monarchy, King Juan Carlos occasionally dropped in on my teaching sessions and hit balls. He could smash them miles and obviously had the inherent talent to become an accomplished player, but he never took up the game.

Both King Leopold of the Belgians and his son, Prince Baudouin, sent for me to give them lessons, and they would have been automatic choices if the crowned heads of Europe had decided to form a golf team.

I am not so sure about Leopold's wife, Princess Lilian. She had the strongest grip I ever saw and I told her: 'You may be a princess but if you hold the club like that you will always be a hooker.' I could have bitten my tongue, as the saying goes, when I realised my gaffe. Fortunately, she was unfamiliar with the expression. Either that or she displayed self-control and forbearance of truly regal proportions.

Role reversal

Golf axiom: in mixed foursomes all husbands become golf professionals. During one tournament I could stand the hectoring and bullying no longer and enquired of the lady how on earth she could put up with being addressed in such terms by her husband. 'Oh, he's not my husband,' she assured me, 'he's my lover.'

An obvious champion

I was working in Cairo when Peter Thomson broke his journey there on his first trip to Britain. The flight from Australia took two days in the lumbering Constellations and, even as a lithe 18-year old, he was extremely stiff when he disembarked. He was travelling with Norman von Nida and they had to go straight to the golf course to play an exhibition match against me and Hassan Hassanein.

Thomson's game immediately caught my attention because of his touch with the short shots. His stiff back meant that his long game was wayward but he scrambled to telling effect, getting the ball up and down so regularly that he reached the turn in par-36. By now the hot sun and the exercise had done their remedial work on his back and he turned on a dazzling display of shot making. If it had been possible to buy shares in that teenager I would have invested every penny I could scrape together.

The spirit of golf

If you were to ask me to recall an incident which sums up the spirit of golf, and professional golf in particular, my mind would instantly go back to a French Open Championship at La Boulie when the South African Harold Henning needed to finish with two fours to share second place

On the 17th hole he pushed his drive slightly and the ball ran in among some leaves. He identified the ball by brand name and number, played to the green and holed out. When he retrieved the ball from the hole he looked carefully and announced: 'This isn't my ball.' It was indeed the right make, Slazenger B51, and the right number, 3, but he was sure it was not his ball. So he effectively disqualified himself and later went back and found his own ball under the leaves.

Harold's honesty meant that the rest of us all moved up a place in the prize list. On the bus taking the players to the airport, we had a whip round and collected virtually the full amount of the second prize and gave it to Harold.

I suppose the amateur equivalent of this incident would be when Bobby Jones called a penalty on himself for an infringement which nobody saw but him. When someone started to compliment him on his action, Jones brusquely cut him short by saying it was like praising a man for not robbing a bank.

Quite so. I might add that in the French Open incident we were not rewarding Harold from refraining from robbing a bank; we simply felt guilty at profiting from his honesty.

Small World

One of the participants in the 1994 Apollo Tour school for new PGA European Tour cardholders, Jonathan Lomas, a very promising young professional, called me to say that he had been going through his grandfather's deed box and had come across a letter from my mother.

The subject matter of that letter took me back to my youth, during the early days of the war. I used to help out on the neighbouring farm and the grateful farmer gave me two gilt pigs. Since the fairways were cut by horse-drawn mowers, we were able to build a pigsty adjoining the stable.

The Lindrick clubhouse was converted into a maternity home during the war and my mother did the catering. She kept the golfers going at weekends by providing snacks in the professional's shop and fed the pigs on the scraps from both establishments. Those two pigs had several litters and so, in the food shortages of wartime, pig breeding became a useful and thriving little sideline.

That letter concerned the sale of the last of the pigs to Jonathan Lomas's grandfather, the local butcher.

You bounder, sir; you've defiled my lady wife!

I feel sure it is true of all golf coaches that teaching is more, much more, than just a way of making a living. The rewards of having former pupils come up to you and say how their golf, and their lives, were transformed by the help you gave them many years before is, literally, beyond price. The satisfaction of giving someone the source of one of life's great pleasures is the stimulus which keeps me teaching long after I should have retired to the river bank with my trout rod.

Very often, however, the ex-pupil who has poured out his gratitude for giving him a lifetime of happiness on the links then hits one with the whammy of a codicil: 'But you have absolutely ruined my wife's swing.'

That, I must say, is hard to take since never in my entire life have I even met the lady in question. What has happened in almost all cases, of course, is that in teaching the man and explaining in patient detail how the swing operates, you create the monster of a self-appointed golf professional who goes home and gives his wife lessons. He may have come to me as a tilter with an unduly upright swing arc which, in due course, I have put right. But you can imagine the havoc he would create if he applied my swing-faulter remedy to a wife whose swing was already excessively flat.

To the best of my knowledge Alexander Pope did not spend a lot of time on the practice ground curing the slices of 17th century golfing tyros but he certainly said it for all golf teachers when he wrote: 'A little learning is a dangerous thing . . .'

1981, Walton Heath:
Ryder Cup selection shenanigans

A strange and testing golf course played the second time round sometimes seems more difficult than it did 'blind'. A similar experience awaited John Jacobs in his second captaincy of Great Britain and Europe in the Ryder Cup match at Walton Heath, Surrey, in September 1981. He had been over the ground before, but now some fiend had slipped in unseen an extra hazard or two where before there had been none.

The United States had selected 'a corker of a side'. A team which, at the start of the 1980s, opened with

Nicklaus, Watson, Floyd, Irwin, Trevino, Nelson and Kite, to say nothing of Miller, Crenshaw and the rest, was clearly going to take some beating. But the European Tour managed to shoot itself in the instep before a ball had been struck.

The difficulties for the home side – and for Jacobs in particular – began with the selection. Looking back now, it was a tragic business. There had been one change in the committee from the body which had picked the last two places in 1979; the German Bernhard Langer, leader now of the order of merit, replacing Ballesteros.

At the time, Ballesteros was at odds with the tournament committee over the payment of appearance money on the tour. As a member of this select community, he was expected to toe the line and refuse any inducements to compete in sponsored events. Yet he had already won the British Open and had triumphed in the US Masters at Augusta in the previous year. He was now in the world league and was well able to command large slices of the sponsors' cash to appear. What irked him – and, as a proud Spaniard, his chagrin was wholly comprehensible – was that his American counterparts at the time, Trevino, Weiskopf and others, were receiving substantial sums to fly over and enter the British tournaments.

Jacobs's position, which he represented in vain to the tournament committee, was unequivocal. 'No appearance money' was acceptable as a rule – provided there were no exceptions. What certainly wasn't right in his judgement was to expect a player of Ballesteros's stature to be denied the chance of getting the cash if leading Americans were able to come over and grab it. He was strongly supported in this stance by Tony Jacklin.

When the selection committee met at Fulford, Yorkshire, at the end of the Benson & Hedges tournament in August 1981 to fill the last two places in the British and European team, there was a marked difference from the position which had obtained in 1979. Neil Coles, from the chair, did not say to Jacobs as he had done two years before 'Come on John, tell us who you want.' He knew quite well who would be the captain's first choice. Jacobs, therefore, put the obvious question to his two colleagues: 'How do you two feel about Seve?'

Coles's answer was an emphatic negative; the Spaniard was in dispute with the tour, he had played little on it that summer and he should not be considered a starter. Langer, having tested the players' opinions and, in a sense, being their representative on the committee, concurred with Coles. His playing colleagues felt that, because Severiano had stayed away from the tour so much with his dispute going on, he should not be selected. Jacobs had himself talked to them and found similar opposition.

The thrust of the conversation was not, as has been suggested, to encourage Ballesteros to settle his differences with the European Tour; psychologically, that would have been a bad move. Rather it was to persuade Severiano to come over and play in two tournaments – Carrolls' Irish Open at Portmarnock and the Benson & Hedges at York. If he would do that, the captain explained, his chances of selection, which Jacobs was so anxious to promote, would at once be enhanced: 'I want you in the team, Seve, but there's little chance of me achieving this unless you are prepared to come over and play in these two events.'

It had been a relatively poor season for Ballesteros. By his exceptional standards, he hadn't been playing well, and spending so much time in the United States in these circumstances had made him depressed. Although the Spaniard said he would think about it, Jacobs was not hopeful. In the event, Ballesteros failed to show up for either competition. His exclusion from the team thus became inevitable. For the captain, it was like having to drive a powerful car across the continent without the use of top gear.

Did you see it?

Watching Arnold Palmer in his heyday was the most compelling of sights. There was nothing scientific about his swing – it relied on one thing . . . power, and lots of it! Arnold was built like a middleweight boxer and gave the ball a fearful crunch. The earth practically shook when he hit the ball.

I'll never forget a great story from when Arnold was playing in the final round of the 1964 Masters with Dave Marr, a witty and charming man who sadly died in 1998. Arnold torpedoed one of his awesome long-iron shots towards the water-guarded 15th green, shooting straight into a low sun. Blinded by the light, he looked to Marr and enquired: 'Did it get over?' to which Marr memorably replied: 'Hell Arnold, your divot got over!' Laying up was never Arnie's style.

An enjoyable and special relationship

The start of my enduring love affair with the United States was in 1955 when I went over to play the American circuit, the highlight of which was a fortuitous pairing with Byron Nelson at Thunderbird in Palm Springs where we were to have the Ryder Cup match. In that match I acquitted myself well enough, two points from two matches, to earn invitations for the Masters for the next two years. Can you believe that I declined each time, with regrets that my lesson book was too full?

In 1972 I heard from an old friend, Ken Bowden, co-editor of my book, *Practical Golf*, and then editor of *Golf Digest* magazine. He invited me to preside over the magazine's first golf school in Phoenix, Arizona. A number of American professionals came along as observers. Afterwards Bert Beuhler, Shelby Futch, Craig and Scott Bunker and the English Pro Donald (Doon) Crawley joined me in the creation of the first John Jacobs Practical Golf Schools. We all worked like mad, but we still had fun.

It was exciting and exacting work building up the 24 locations for the John Jacobs Golf Schools (in 1995 more than 1,000 classes took place). When the toil and travel became too taxing for me, Shelby, to my great good fortune, stepped in and took over the reins as my partner and later as the owner of the company. I am extremely proud of all those guys who worked so hard helping me build up the business. I owe so much to them, and to America.

By Royal command

I was preparing for one of my regular coaching sessions with the German teams when I received word that, since the February weather in Spain, where we customarily held our sessions, had been disappointing in recent years, they had switched to Morocco. I flew out a day early and when I reported to the Royal Dar Es Salaam club at Rabat I was immediately invited to join the sister of King Hussain II for a game of golf.

The next day I was busy with my tutorial duties on the practice ground when a senior government official approached and informed me that I must make myself available every afternoon to play golf with His Majesty. My expression must have conveyed some hint of my unspoken thoughts, because the official made it eminently clear that Morocco's continued welcome to myself and the German teams was dependent upon my embracing this signal honour without demur.

Arrangements were quickly made for the German teams to be suitably looked after during my enforced afternoon absences. My services were not required every day but when we did play, on the King's private nine-hole course within the grounds of his royal palace – one of several such courses around the country, I might add – the experience was quite fantastic, using that overworked word in its literal sense of dreamlike fantasy.

His Majesty started by entering a small tent and making his choice from a selection of some 30 pairs of golf shoes on display. A truck containing 20 sets of golf clubs followed our progress around the course.

The King is a great enthusiast for the game and a fair striker of the ball, but it is difficult to assess his handicap level. His golfing companions perforce are drawn from the ranks of ministers, diplomats and high government officials, all men with an acute appreciation of which side their bread is buttered and, accordingly, most generous in ideas of what constitutes a royal 'gimme.' There is, in short, no such thing for the King as a second putt in this school.

The King is a wizard out of the rough, a fact not entirely unconnected with the retinue of some 50 or 60 solicitous attendants: security men, flunkeys, functionaries, fore-caddies and the like. They made sure his ball was always nicely teed up. I am sure that the King does not command such favourable consideration. He would surely get more genuine satisfaction from his golf if he played in a hard-nosed fourball which insisted on seeing every putt into the hole and no hanky panky in the rough. But being who he is, his is the only form of golf available to him.

Urgent affairs of State dictated how many holes the King played. When the game stopped and the King departed, we all adjourned to a large marquee in the grounds. Here were served mountains of couscous, whole roasted sheep, barons of beef, pigeon pies, a profusion of fruits, and steaming hot mint tea served from silver pitchers.

One corner of the tent was set aside especially for the visiting English *professeur de golf*. I had to make do with caviar and Veuve Cliquot!

Fighting for the Big Ball

John Jacobs had concluded early in the 1950s that the Americans' generally superior, and altogether firmer, striking was the product of their adoption of the large 1.68-inch ball two decades before. He had repeated his opinion both in the press and in talks at golfing gatherings throughout the 1950s and into the 1960s. With Henry Cotton, Leonard Crawley, the British amateur and golf correspondent of the *Daily Telegraph* and *Field*, and a few other contemporaries in the United Kingdom, he never missed an opportunity of urging upon the authorities the adoption of the large version in the tournaments. He had summed up his arguments in his first book. The words formed the basis of an article which was first published in the magazine *Golfing* in 1959:

'I am convinced that it is high time we came into line with our American friends and conceded that theirs is the better-sized ball to play with . . .The real point is that if the large ball is not quite 'middled' it flies considerably less far than the small one from the same sort of stroke . . . This is a good thing. It may be the reason why the best American players use an action which keeps the club blade squared for longer in the hitting area as opposed to the more common method in this country in which the wrist-flick and roll have been overemphasised.

'This type of 'blade square for longer through the ball' we call 'driving the ball' . . . I am absolutely certain . . . that to drive the ball is by far the sounder method . . . Generalising then, *we* flick the ball; *they* drive the ball . . . To get results, the US large-size ball has to be driven; and, therefore, right from the start, it encourages a sounder method. I very much believe the weekend golfer would eventually find it an easier ball to play with and one which would sooner or later automatically improve his game.'

The great Sam Snead once made a telling aside to Henry Cotton when he was playing at Wentworth. Snead was then well past his prime and the British 'bullet' was still in use in the professional tournaments. 'You know, Henry,' he said, 'I like playing golf over here in my old age. I can miss this small ball of yours and still get away with it.'

For the tournament player, the large US ball required more exacting control; yet, for the average golfer, it had undoubted benefits – which is why the Americans adopted it in the first place. Market research at Athlon's centres confirmed that the patrons preferred it.

Predictably, all through the controversy, the British manufacturers kept up a barrage of opposition to suggestions for a change. While they made the 1.62 bullet well, they were fully aware that the 1.68-inch ball made in small quantities in Britain fell far short of the first-class American product. It would be expensive and take a long time to close the gap.

In the end, spurred on by Cotton, Jacobs, Dai Rees, Tommy Horton and others in this country, and overseas by the likes of Tommy Armour, the old silver fox, who had seen it all in the States, Palmer, Nicklaus and Player, the British PGA rejected the soft option and, in the mid-1960s, plumped irrevocably for the 1.68-inch ball in its tournaments.

As is explained below, for the first time, the whole hullabaloo need never have happened.

One evening in 1966, Roger Wethered and his wife were dining at my home in London. The arguments and counter-arguments about the ball were still at their height. The PGA had only then just taken its decision in favour of the 1.68-inch size and given the lead which others would later follow. With Cyril Tolley, Wethered had formed half the pair in what, in the Golden Age of amateur golf after World War I, had become know as the 'Tolley-Wethered era'. Historically, it matched the 'Jones era' in the United States. Roger could play golf, and behind a winning modesty, there lay a deep knowledge of the game. When he did talk about it seriously – which was seldom – it was generally always in private.

Wethered had tied with Jock Hutchinson for the 1921

Open Championship at St Andrews. He lost the 18-hole replay the next day – and, with it, a promised day's cricket in the south. He won the Amateur Championship at Deal two years later and stayed in Moore-Brabazon's (later Lord Brabazon) house at Sandwich Bay for it. The chambermaid called him with a pot of tea at 7.30 on the morning of the final, ensuring that the curtains in the bedroom were fully drawn back before she closed the door. An hour later, his host went up to find out why his eminent guest hadn't come down to breakfast. The tea beside the bed was untouched and cold. Wethered was still doggo.

After his victory, he was twice runner-up in the championship, the second time to Bobby Jones at St Andrews in 1930, Jones's Grand Slam year. In his prime Wethered was as good an iron player as there was in the game, amateur or professional. Had Jacobs been about in those days, he might well have fixed up Roger's somewhat wayward driving, and then he would have been well-nigh invincible, for he had a sensitive short game, a silken putting stroke and just the right, unflappable temperament for a champion.

The point is that Wethered knew about golf at first hand – an authoritative hand at that. He did not talk openly about the ball for he was not much enamoured of controversy, but he was an incorrigible protagonist of the larger version. He was well aware that I was active in its support.

As the diners left the table, he put a hand on my arm. 'If we could sit down for five minutes,' he said, 'I could tell you privately about the ball.' He then recounted his depressing story. A note which I made the next day and then locked away serves as an *aide memoire*.

Soon after the Second World War, Wethered had been made chairman of a small working party at St Andrews, set up, as he put it, 'to look into the question of the ball'. In particular, it was to examine the difficulty which arose from the United States using one size of ball and the United Kingdom, and its followers, another. The outcome of the study was still quite fresh in Wethered's mind.

'We did our work quickly. It was obvious that, if there was to be a change, then, in fairness to the manufacturers, notice should be given as soon as possible. Their factories were turning over from wartime to peacetime production and getting ready to meet the demand for golf balls, which were then in short supply.

'My group came up with one principal recommendation – that we should adopt the American specification for the ball which the USGA had decided upon in the early 1930s, 1.68 inches in diameter and 1.62 ounces in weight. It wasn't difficult to get agreement and I'm quite sure we were right. I was convinced of it myself. It wasn't that we were blindly following the Americans; there were playing advantages with the 1.68-inch ball which were denied with the smaller one.'

It was now well into 1946: 'One day, Monty Pease (JW Beaumont Pease, an England and Oxford player, then Chairman of Lloyds Bank), who was the chairman of the general committee of the R&A, saw me in the City of London. (Wethered had stockbroking and finance interests in the City of London.) He explained that, as the Walker Cup match was being played at St Andrews the following spring and representatives of the USGA would be coming over for talks with the R&A, it would be courteous to them to defer a decision on the ball. It would be right to talk things over with them first. They wanted to carry the Americans with us, the aim of the two governing bodies always being to try to march in step.

'I said I thought this was quite wrong on timing. A different situation would arise by then with the manufacturers. They had to get on and meet the demand for balls, and once they were geared up to produce the small ball in large numbers, they would never want to change over to something else. It would cost them money. I said that if it was really felt necessary to consult the Americans then surely someone could go over there and talk to them. I was fairly sure the arguments about the larger ball weren't understood and its importance was mostly missed.

'In the end, I allowed Monty to talk me out of it. I should never have done so. Although I say it, I feel certain I would have got the backing to carry the thing had I dug in my heels. But I didn't want to go against the general committee and make difficulties. I am afraid, looking back, it was a terrible mistake. The opportunity had been lost. Now we'd get all this row . . .'

It is easy to see now why Wethered was so certain that a fundamental misjudgement had been made. He knew that the use of the bigger ball promoted better, more solid striking and greater accuracy close to the green. By comparison with the advance of United States golf during the subsequent 30 years or so, the mistake put us at a disadvantage. Beyond that, it compelled Jacobs and a few of his enlightened followers to mount and win a campaign in the 1960s which need never have been fought. But the effects of that victory were far reaching.

It is only in the last few years that the results of the adoption of the big ball in European golf have truly begun to work through. There has been an all round improvement in the first-class game. A new generation of players has grown up with the ball since childhood and thereby enjoyed an advantage which its predecessors never knew – and should never have been denied.

Winston Churchill once described the Second World War as the 'unnecessary war'. Roger Wethered could well have said the same of the conflict which bedevilled the British game in the third quarter of the 20th century.*

---

* It is worth noting that Raymond Floyd, the 1986 US Open champion, one of the world's greats and long conversant with British and European golf, was asked by *Sunday Express* correspondent Alan Tyne, in California in January 1987, why the gap between the United States and Britain and Europe had narrowed so perceptibly in recent years. He gave 'the introduction of the bigger, American ball' as his first reason. 'This,' he added, 'automatically made them better strikers once they got the hang of it.'

John Jacobs, 2001.